DELIBERATE
RECEIVING

DELIBERATE
RECEIVING

Finally, the Universe
Makes Some Freakin' Sense!

Melody Fletcher

HAY HOUSE

Carlsbad, California • New York City • London • Sydney
Johannesburg • Vancouver • Hong Kong • New Delhi

First published and distributed in the United Kingdom by:
Hay House UK Ltd, Astley House, 33 Notting Hill Gate, London W11 3JQ
Tel: +44 (0)20 3675 2450; Fax: +44 (0)20 3675 2451
www.hayhouse.co.uk

Published and distributed in the United States of America by:
Hay House Inc., PO Box 5100, Carlsbad, CA 92018-5100
Tel: (1) 760 431 7695 or (800) 654 5126; Fax: (1) 760 431 6948 or (800) 650 5115
www.hayhouse.com

Published and distributed in Australia by:
Hay House Australia Ltd, 18/36 Ralph St, Alexandria NSW 2015
Tel: (61) 2 9669 4299; Fax: (61) 2 9669 4144; www.hayhouse.com.au

Published and distributed in the Republic of South Africa by:
Hay House SA (Pty) Ltd, PO Box 990, Witkoppen 2068
info@hayhouse.co.za; www.hayhouse.co.za

Published and distributed in India by:
Hay House Publishers India, Muskaan Complex, Plot No.3, B-2,
Vasant Kunj, New Delhi 110 070
Tel: (91) 11 4176 1620; Fax: (91) 11 4176 1630; www.hayhouse.co.in

Distributed in Canada by:
Raincoast Books, 2440 Viking Way, Richmond, B.C. V6V 1N2
Tel: (1) 604 448 7100; Fax: (1) 604 270 7161; www.raincoast.com

A catalogue record for this book is available from the British Library.

ISBN: 978-1-78180-494-0

Interior illustrations © James Steidl/Thinkstock

Printed in the UK by TJ International Ltd, Padstow, Cornwall.

For my mom.

If I'm the apple, you're the tree.

I'm glad I didn't fall that far.

Contents

Acknowledgements

This book didn't happen in a vacuum. It's the culmination of a lifetime of lessons learned, and something many people contributed to directly or indirectly.

First and foremost, I want to thank my clients and readers, the Happy Shiny Puppy Army. Without your loyalty, dedication and awesome feedback over the years, this book would not have happened. Without your questions, and ability to hear the answers I'm able to access, I'd really just be a weirdo with a megaphone shouting into an oblivious crowd. You are the reason this book exists. You are the reason I do what I do. Thank you for letting me slap you with enlightenment and love, and for always laughing at my juvenile and ridiculous metaphors. And poop jokes. Let's not forget the poop jokes.

I'd also like to thank my sister and Business Manager (Happy Shiny Puppy Wrangler), Tina Fletcher. As kids, I never would've imagined that we'd be working together some day and yet, here we are. Holy crap, right? Your support, dedication and friendship mean so much to me. Without you, Deliberate Receiving wouldn't be where it is today! I honestly couldn't do what I do without you. I can't wait to see where we go next! And yes, I'm fully aware that this acknowledgement (in writing!) will make you cry. This means I win. Your move, sis.

A huge shout out must go to Amy Kiberd, my commissioning editor at Hay House, for not only recognizing something in me and my blog, and talking me into publishing my book, but also babysitting me through my embarrassing first time author freak outs with such humor and grace. You do know that this book is just the first, right? I hope you realize what you've gotten yourself into.

Another special thanks to my excellent editor Sandy Draper, whose enormous skill and happy shiny attitude were a perfect match to my style. Thank you for making this process so easy on me. Your feedback was invaluable as we found metaphors and analogies that worked for both UK and US audiences (thank God poop metaphors are universally understood!). And also a special thanks to your hubby for confirming that people across the pond do know who MacGyver is.

I'd also like to acknowledge the entire Hay House team: Reid Tracy, Michelle Pilley, Jo Burgess, Tom Cole, and Jessica Gibson (and anyone I missed! Sorry! You're all awesome!), for basically being the best publishing team ever. I really feel like I've been welcomed into a family of highly skilled publishing ninjas. Thank you.

And finally, I'd like to thank my mom, best friend and mentor, Helen Fletcher. You're the original coach, whether you want to believe it or not. Yes. You are. Thank you for always believing in me and being willing to see who I really was all along. Not to mention the whole giving birth to me thing. You got me started in writing all those years ago at six years old, when you'd give me one sentence to start me off and I'd go and write a story. I suspect this was a great tactic to get me to be quiet for a while, but it still worked. In other words, this is really all your fault.

I'm so looking forward to seeing where this journey takes us all. This is just the beginning people. Don't you forget it.

Are You Ready to Wake Up?

Well hey there, stranger! Welcome to *Deliberate Receiving*! If you're reading this book, it likely means that you've been searching for answers to life's biggest questions: Who are we? Why are we here? How do I win the lottery? How do I get my ass to fit into my skinny jeans, and – like Mick Jagger – why have I so far been unable to get any satisfaction? You've been taught to work hard, play only once you've gotten your homework done, eat dessert last, keep your head down, do what you're told and play by rules that often don't make sense to you. You were also taught that if you did all these things like a good little human being, you'd get rewarded with security, stability and possibly even a teensy-weensy bit of happiness (it really isn't a big goal in our society, no matter what the beer commercials say).

Only now, having done everything 'right', having played by the rules, you find yourself lacking a certain something. Call it passion, call it joy, call it awesomeness, call it a job that doesn't suck and a boss who isn't a total douchebag. No matter what is missing, you've likely tried all the conventional methods of bringing about change: working really hard, bitching about it to everyone you know, finding others online who will agree that your situation is totally sucky and tell you about their even suckier lives, playing the numbers game (applying for a ton of jobs, trying online dating because even a blind chicken finds corn every once in a while, am I right?) but, alas, nothing has worked.

Well, my Happy Shiny Puppy in training, that's all about to change.

Let me assure you that you're in the right place. Actually, to be completely honest, you've always been in the right place. It's just that now (the manifestation of this book into your reality is the sign that you're ready!), you're about to be in the really fun place – the place where your life actually begins to work the way you want it to. You're about to head from Dissatisfactionville (or Suckytown, Fearton, Crapolaville, take your pick) to Awesometown. This is where your questions finally get answered. This is where you finally understand how the Universe works, who you really are, what you truly want, why you haven't gotten it so far and, most importantly, exactly what you need to do to get it.

This is not theory. This is practical, immediately implementable information that you can use to change your life for the better. Wait. Screw just *better*. You can change your life for the awesomer, for the spectacular-er, for the… OK you get the point, so I'll stop making up words now. (I'm lying. I'm totally going to keep making up words.)

And no – let's put this baby to rest right now – it's not just about thinking pretty, pretty thoughts and then waiting for your life to fix itself magically. It's about taking control of your life, your entire reality, in a way you've never done before. It's about doing what actually works, so you can make fast, lasting changes to your life. It's about getting what you truly want. It's about becoming so freaking happy that you annoy all your friends and family with your new-found giddiness (can't wait for that one, can you?).

I do have one caveat for you, however. This book isn't so much about showing you how to manifest a Ferrari or a pile of cash or a gorgeous hottie to marry, as it is about changing your entire life and becoming who you really are, who you were always meant to be. Don't get me wrong, all of those *things* are totally great but, as you'll discover, the purpose of life is not to have a fancy car or to beat the neighbours in a game of one-upmanship. You are here to experience so much more than that. So. Much. More. You're here to have your cake and eat it, too. (I've never understood that saying. What's the purpose of having cake, if you can't freaking eat it?)

This book isn't just going to give you a few tools and show you how to use them. That would be like showing you how to use a hammer. Now you can pound nails into boards, which is great, if your life's dream is to run around fixing loose boards. What this book will do is teach you how to design and build any structure, like a house, so you'll know when and how to use that hammer, what that hammer actually does and why it's sometimes not the best tool to use. After all, if you're working with screws, a hammer is going to be pretty useless. You're actually going to learn how reality works and how you can construct it, so you can build anything you want. It's like learning how to cook, versus just learning one recipe, or learning how to build a company versus how to fill in a spreadsheet, or, for you Harry Potter fans, learning how to use magic versus how to do one measly spell.

Of course, learning how to build a house is a little bit more involved than learning how to use a hammer, and learning to become who you really are will require a little more time and effort than using one manifesting technique. The payoff is that this will *change your whole life* for the better, in ways that you can't even imagine yet. And the best part is that you already know how to do all this; I'm just going to be reminding you of what you've forgotten and helping you to make sense of what you already know.

This book is intended to be a sort of technical manual for reality.

- **Part I** introduces the basics of how reality works, why we're here, why we forgot who we really are, and how manifestations actually come about.

- **Part II** goes much, much deeper into the mechanism of reality; this is where you'll discover the nitty-gritty details of managing your energy. This is also where you'll begin to understand yourself and the world in an entirely new way. You'll realize why people (including you) behave the way they do, even when that behaviour is damaging and, most importantly, how to let go finally and permanently of any reactions, ideas and beliefs that aren't working for you. You'll also learn how to figure out what it is you really want, so you'll never again try to build a doghouse when what you actually want is a mansion. You'll finally understand how and why any of the tools you've ever heard of work, as well as why they often *don't* work. You'll never again try to use a hammer when what you really need is a screwdriver.

So, are you ready to begin? I only ask because once you know this stuff, you can't un-know it. Once you've peeked behind the curtain and seen the workings of the machine, you can't ever go back to being obliviously unhappy. Never again will you be able to blame other people or outside circumstances for the fact that you don't like your life. When you *know* that you have the power to manifest what you want, *anything* you want, and exactly how to do that, you can't ever again stick your head in the sand and hope things will just magically get better, or demand that others change so that you can be happy.

I'm giving you the keys to the car and teaching you how to drive it; but you still have to turn over the ignition and put the pedal to the metal. In other words, you're going to have to be the one that implements all of this knowledge and understanding in your own life. If you're willing to do that, you're about to take the first steps to becoming what I call a Happy Shiny Puppy – an infinitely joyful, playful, loving, open and authentic being who doesn't take life too seriously and is so happy that others become happy just by being in the vicinity.

If you're ready to wake up, if you're sure that you actually want to know the secrets of the Universe, you'd better strap yourself in my Puppies, because here we go.

Part 1

THE BASICS

Chapter 1

Who the Hell is Melody Fletcher?

At this point, you may be asking yourself who the hell I am and what qualifies me to write this book? And you'd be totally right to do that. After all, you don't want to just believe any old weirdo who comes along and tells you they understand how reality works. Some of those people are kind of creepy.

You should question your teachers. In fact, you should question everything, but we'll get to that a bit later. First, I'm going to give you a little glimpse of my journey and how I've come to know what I know. I promise not to get too weird or woo-woo on your butt (although I do speak everything from 'woo' to 'woo-woo', this book will keep it more on the 'woo' side).

The making of a workaholic

I've always had the ability to read energy, although for most of my life I didn't know that this is what I was doing. I could tell what people were feeling. I was and am what many people call an 'empath': someone with a natural talent for reading other people's energy. Everyone has this ability. If you've ever had a gut feeling about someone or something, you've read energy. If reading energy were like reading music, an empath would be a naturally gifted musician, someone who can just pick up an instrument and play it without ever having taken a lesson.

The only problem is that, unlike musical ability, most people don't recognize energy-reading abilities, or at least they didn't when I was growing up. So, when you're a little girl freaking out about the massive rage someone in front of her is feeling, the adults in the vicinity don't tend to be sympathetic. After all, there's nothing to freak out about, right? Being empathic in a world that doesn't understand how energy works and doesn't even recognize non-physical energy for the most part can present some challenges. You end up having to navigate the labyrinth that is other people's emotions and fears, not really knowing they're not yours, doing your best to ignore the avalanche of 'extra' information you're getting, but which no one else seems to recognize, in an effort not to be the weird one. (This never works. The weirdness always squishes out.)

In my case, I did my best to shut down that extra data stream and fit into what people call 'normal' society. Of course, you can't really ever shut it down, but you can ignore it, and so that's what I did – but to my own detriment. Like most empaths of my generation and before, I had no idea what was happening. I just knew I was strange. I also couldn't understand why other people weren't freaking out, that they weren't getting the same information that I was. It didn't seem to bother them when someone's words didn't match their energy (they were lying to themselves and others). I perceived the world to be a profoundly confusing, and often unfair, place, where people thought one thing and did another, perceived attacks when there were none (but from which they defended themselves just the same) and punished each other for their mutual unhappiness (perpetuating it).

On top of all of this emotional mayhem, I was also born with the strong desire to help others; to make them feel better. Pretty much from day one, I made it my mission to cheer up everyone around me, and took it very personally when it didn't work. If their happiness was my job, then their unhappiness represented my failure. Every time an adult in my presence had a bad day, I took it as a sign that I sucked at my main purpose in life.

Now, while part of my life's work *is* to help others, I had completely misunderstood what that meant and what it entailed, leading me to feel obligated from a very young age to help anyone and everyone, no matter whether it felt good, completely depleted me or even worked. I was willing to sacrifice myself and let others completely drain me for even the tiniest chance of making them feel better. If this sounds at all familiar, don't worry, I will be showing you later how to knock that crap right the hell off.

This sense of failure, of not being good enough at something that was a part of my purpose, is what led me to become a total workaholic. Not only was it a wonderful distraction from my self-deprecating thoughts, but also I figured if I just worked hard enough I could finally prove my worthiness. (Spoiler alert: that doesn't work).

I started off by washing dishes in our family's German deli aged 13 and progressed to managing multimillion-dollar restaurants in San Francisco during my college years. After nearly having a nervous breakdown from working 120 hours a week (yes, seriously, I only slept every other day), due to a complete and utter inability to say no (this is called 'setting boundaries'), I left that town and profession, along with an abusive romantic relationship, to seek greener pastures and an easier life. (I don't blame you San Francisco and I will always have a smooshy place for you in my heart!) After taking a bit of a rest and recovering my sanity, I was divinely guided (my manicurist suggested it) to go to Las Vegas. My insistence on doing everything the hard way left me virtually homeless after a few months there (I had to pay my dues, after all), but I eventually decided to become a dealer (cards, not drugs, I swear).

An empath in crisis

Living in Vegas was pretty cool, I won't lie to you, but when you're sensitive to energy, it can also be a devastatingly negative place. This goes double for those working in casinos in a profession that basically entails getting yelled at by drunk people whose money you just took. (They don't tend to like that very much. Go figure.) I was earning the most money I ever had, but the desperation, depression and self-loathing of those around me really started to take its toll. It got so bad that every time the energy overwhelmed me, my body hit the reset button and I would faint. That's right, I was a blackjack dealer who couldn't keep from passing out. It happened so regularly that my pit boss actually caught me mid-fall on several occasions. (If only I'd been conscious to experience the chivalry.)

As if that wasn't a big enough hint, my health also started to fail in other ways. Despite a punishing three-hour session at the gym every day and a ridiculously strict diet (I do not recommend this, I was totally nuts – can you say 'control freak'?), I began to gain weight rapidly and sometimes was so fatigued that I couldn't get out of bed. Some 30 (I kid you not) doctors later and I was no closer to figuring out what was wrong with me. Nowadays, they'd probably label me as having chronic fatigue syndrome, but that didn't exist back then, so they just told me that I was obviously making up all my symptoms and I should maybe see a shrink.

Tired, depressed and out of answers, I quit Vegas and the casino business and moved to Germany to get the best rehabilitation there is – a mother's love. Although I wasn't keen on seeing any more doctors, I did eventually manage to find a naturopath who not only believed that I was telling the truth (I can't tell you how much of a relief that was), but believed she could help me. Six gruelling months of treatments later, I had my energy back. In the meantime, though, I'd gone ahead and resumed my workaholic ways! Because as long as you CAN work, you might as well, right? (Sarcasm alert!)

Never one to waste time, I was hired by a German distributor of telecommunications components just two weeks after my arrival. Originally, my job was to answer the phone. Two and half years later, I was visiting multibillion-dollar conglomerates as a sales representative for the company's fibre-optic components line. (Admit it. You're *totally* impressed). I've always been successful at pretty much everything I've done, at least by conventional standards. I always got promoted quickly, earned a lot of money, was given a great deal of responsibility and received huge amounts of praise. What I wasn't, was happy. And when I realized that, once again, I'd given into workaholic temptation, I decided to do something completely different.

I attempt to live the perfect life

I quit my job and backpacked around Europe for four months. (Take that, corporate life!) I was going to teach English, be a hippie, possibly become a dive-master, stop shaving my armpits (OK, not really), live on an island somewhere, have sand from the beach permanently lodged in my body's nooks and crannies, and drink everything with a little umbrella in it. Even my morning coffee. I did pretty much just that for four months. My plan was to finish the trip in Barcelona, Spain, get my English Teaching certificate and then continue my vagabonding ways around the globe. I got as far as getting the certificate, but after a month in Barcelona, I found myself drawn to staying there for just a little longer.

After a year of teaching English and German, and partying harder than I ever did in my college days (I was determined not to fall into old patterns and figured if I acted differently, I'd be different. Spoiler alert: That doesn't work either.), I realized that I loved Spain, and Barcelona in particular, but HATED teaching languages. I felt as though my soul was being slowly sucked out of my body. The only other job I'd ever had that rivalled this one in terms of boredom was working in retail: standing around all day, waiting for people to buy something. You see, I needed to have a fast-paced job, something to distract me from all the stuff I didn't want to deal with; the stuff I didn't think I *could* deal with. So, I decided to get a 'real' job.

Enough is enough

Five years later, I was the Operations Head of a technology service centre for one of the largest financial institutions in the world, based in Barcelona. I was, once again, working 18-hour days and slowly but surely killing myself. At this point you may be thinking that I'm a bit of a slow learner and you'd be totally right. My patterns were so ingrained it was ridiculously easy for me to fall back into them. Taking away my 18-hour workdays was a bit like taking away a heroin addict's fix. I couldn't just decide to stop. I couldn't simply *act* differently (no one can). Something else had to happen in order to effect real change.

One really good thing about this super-corporate job was that I was in charge of my own centre, which meant I was able to run it (within limits) the way I wanted. I couldn't really give people as much money as they deserved, but I was able to create a much more positive, infinitely more productive and spectacularly successful work environment by applying many of the principles and techniques I'll be sharing with you in this book. Without being consciously aware of it, I was teaching people about energy all along.

After five and a half years of bureaucracy, poor health and never-ending stress, I'd finally had enough. When the company ordered me to lay off all the people I'd personally hired, trained and nurtured, I decided to leave right along with them. Although I'd already managed to make huge strides in terms of my work addiction – I'd reduced my working day to eight hours, becoming MORE successful in the process – I was physically and emotionally exhausted and heartbroken. Shutting down the teams I had helped to create was a bit like killing my own baby (it was also, in my eyes, a very bad business decision). The only thing that brought me relief in that moment was to get out.

My moment of awakening

And that's when my life finally truly changed. Instead of taking a one- or two-week holiday, which served as nothing but a Band-Aid – a relief valve that allowed a bit of the pressure to escape – for the first time in my life, I made some serious time for myself. You see, even when I'd backpacked, I'd kept myself super busy: I changed cities every three days, ran around sightseeing and fell into bed completely exhausted every night. I left no time to *really think*.

This time, I took off an entire year and planned to do absolutely nothing. I actually made space in my life. I considered it my sabbatical. The first three months were spent in a kind of coma-like state. I slept a lot, watched some funny shows, listened to inspirational audios by Abraham and Bashar (two channelled entities), meditated and spent some real, quality time with my thoughts. As the stress left my body, all the damage I'd been doing to it over the years became apparent. My back seized up; my foot went numb for two weeks; I had a pinched nerve in my hip. But instead of taking painkillers and just pushing through it, the way I'd always done in the past, I actually rested. I allowed my body to heal. Each ailment took its turn and left. I was purging all the stress out of my system.

After three months, as I was sitting in meditation one day, the penny dropped. I suddenly understood how the Universe worked. This was what many people call a 'spiritual awakening'. For me it was the first of many. In that moment, it was as though a veil had been drawn back and I was given access to the Universe's machine room. I couldn't yet understand what all the levers and blinking lights were for, I couldn't comprehend all the details, but the basics had become clear. And oh man, was it exciting.

In that one moment, it was as though everything I'd known since I was a child came back into my conscious understanding. I saw the underlying reasons why people acted the way they did, why we hurt each other and what it is that we really want. I understood how reality is shaped, and how we can control it, how we DO control it and why most people seem consistently to create what they fear the most. It was like being handed a technical manual for how to be truly human, how to realize my greatest potential and how to actually get the life I'd always wanted. You'd think that all this information would've come in with a bang, hitting me like a ton of bricks. But it was much more like remembering something I'd long forgotten but always sort of knew. Instead of a 'Holy crap! Who knew?' moment, it felt more like 'Oh yeah… that's right!'

A few months later, I found myself in the Peruvian rainforest, working with a shaman, participating in ayahuasca ceremonies – ayahuasca is a potent jungle vine and powerful plant teacher. I'd always been sensitive to energy, I was even already able to sort of communicate with my spirit guides, but my connection was suddenly ripped wide open. It was as though I'd gone from a 1930s telephone connection to high-speed fibre-optic video. I was given access to the Universal database and every question I'd ever had was answered. And, most profoundly, I was shown in nitty-gritty detail how not even a second of my life had ever been wasted. Every moment I'd experienced had been perfect and had led to me being exactly where I was. None of it had been a mistake, not even the difficult parts. Of course, the suffering had not been necessary as far as the Universe was concerned (that was all me), but none of it had been a mistake.

These insights led me to an even deeper understanding of why people feel the way they do, why they think, act and react the way they do. I was able to review not only my own life in a way that made sense (along with all the people I'd encountered on my various workaholic adventures), but the lives of others, as well. And what's more, I was able to explain it.

I've always loved breaking complex systems down into simple components so that others could easily understand them. I've always been a teacher. When I was seven, I would teach my stuffed animals and later, when I was in the corporate world, I spent a lot of time training others to be much more effective in their roles. But now, I had found the ultimate topic, at least in my view.

This crap really works!

I stopped blaming the crappy jobs, the shitty bosses, the government and even myself. In fact, I stopped blaming altogether. I took responsibility and full control of my destiny. (Blame and responsibility are not the same thing, something I'll explore in detail later in this book.) I started making changes on an energetic level instead of trying to change things through action. And my life started to quickly and, even better, *easily* improve. I understood fully why I had finally been able to reduce my workday successfully towards the end of my corporate career, and was able to give up having to work non-stop. I brought balance into my life; I built an awesome six-figure business without ever investing in advertising, lost over 100lb, stopped dating abusive men and started dating amazing guys, learnt to truly love myself and turned into a Happy Shiny Puppy. And, best of all, I now get to help people every day without depleting myself. In fact, it energizes me.

I have the ability to raise myself to a very high vibration (this term will become clear shortly), connect with my clients' higher selves (who they really are) and translate that energy back to them. This is a type of channelling, although I don't 'leave the room' or go into trance, so I prefer the term 'translating'. As I put all my focus on a person, I am able to feel their vibration and the emotions that accompany them (even if they, themselves, are not aware of how they feel), and receive the energy of a person's Higher Self, translating it into words (I take full credit for the sarcasm, though). I get to connect with who they really are (which is always an amazing, powerful creator) and help them find the path to what it is they really want (an awesome, joyful life beyond their wildest dreams). I get to be a conduit for their self-empowerment, hold the vision of their true potential and, more importantly, help them see it too.

In order to do this, first I had to connect with who I really am, which is what this book will teach you how to do. My life now is full of joy, awesomeness, love and adventure, and it's only getting better and better each day. I wrote this book (or 'translated' this book), because I want the same for you.

When I launched my blog and, a year later, my coaching practice and began to apply what I'd remembered (and helped others to do the same) and teach how the Universal Machine actually works and how to apply it, my clients' lives began to change dramatically for the better, too. The fact is that much of what I do is really about helping others to strip away the BS we've been taught about how reality works and who we really are (which some call the 'Higher Self'), and to remember what we've always inherently known.

Since then, I've worked directly with hundreds of clients and have reached hundreds of thousands more through my blog, and have had the great pleasure and honour of witnessing them deliberately receiving the lives they've always wanted. Like me, they've left behind depression, sadness, workaholism, false obligation, a sense of failure, self-criticism, never-ending stress, the feeling of being trapped, loneliness, powerlessness and anything else that stands in the way of pure joy.

These are real people, living in the real world. No one I know has changed their life by sitting on a mountain for six months and chanting 'Om!' These are people with jobs and businesses, partners who don't necessarily have any interest in inner work, kids, PTA meetings, judge-y neighbours and chocolate addictions. What's more, these are intelligent people, well educated, with strong minds that won't just accept any old theory on blind faith. Any new paradigm that has a chance of being adopted into practice has to make sense, dammit, or it's going in the bin. In short, these are my people.

Not one of these individuals was required to give up the comfort of their iThingy, go vegan, hug trees (you may want to, but you don't *have to*), talk to their partner about their chi, or switch to green tea against their will. The point of all this 'work' is to get the life that you truly want, not the life that some guru (or the TV or your mother) thinks you should want. And that's exactly what you get when you finally understand how the Universe functions and begin to live your life according to a completely different set of rules (the ones that actually work). You get the life YOU want.

I know this sounds like a lofty promise. But trust me, whatever challenges you're currently facing, I've been there. Crappy job? Check. Shitty relationships? Check. Weight and health problems? Check and check. Poverty? Checkaroony. Rejection? Checkadoodle. Not being understood/being the weirdo/

discrimination? Checkilicious. Yeah, I've got you covered. But not only was I able to leave all of those experiences behind, I've helped tons of real-life people do the same. You can actually get the life you've always dreamed of. And it's not even that hard. You just need to understand how reality actually works, that's all. Or rather, you have to remember.

And that's where I come in – I'm here to help remind you of what you already know, what you've always known deep down. It's that voice calling 'Bullshit!' several times a day. Like me, you may have done your best to ignore that little voice, to shut it up, but the very fact that you're holding this book proves that you weren't all that successful. *Thank Gawd!*

So, if you're ready to have some updated ancient knowledge dropped on you, if you're ready to be (lovingly) slapped with enlightenment, if you're ready to remember *who* you really are and *how* the game actually works, keep on reading.

Let's start with the basics, shall we?

Chapter 2

Welcome to the Game

At some point, you've probably come across the idea that 'you create your own reality'. And, sure, that sounds great in theory, but how exactly is that supposed to work? I mean, if you actually do create your own reality, if you create everything that's in your life, then why in the hell is your world filled with a bunch of crap you don't want? Wouldn't you have created it to be more awesome? Wouldn't you have created a life that's easier, more full of joy and with way fewer idiots? Well, of course you would have, if only you knew what you were doing, if only you knew how it actually worked. But you were trained out of that knowledge, encouraged to forget, and therefore weren't consciously shaping your reality, which is exactly why you're reading this book.

The truth is you do create your own reality; you've just been doing it by default. We all have. And it's not because you're not capable of more; it's just that you've been living according to some very limiting 'rules' based on some very limiting and mostly false observations and assumptions.

Imagine entering a world full of vending machines. Only you can't see what's in them, and there are no labels on the buttons. You begin to push some of those buttons randomly, and stuff starts squirting out – some of it very tasty (wanted) and a lot of it really gross (unwanted). After a while, you may begin to notice some patterns; for example, every time you push a certain button, you get this nasty mushy paste that tastes like old feet. So, you mark that button with a red dot, and don't push it any more. When other newbies join you, you pass on what you've learnt so far. You teach them which buttons to avoid. Those newbies then teach other newbies and so on, until after a while, the newest newbies don't even know why they're avoiding the buttons with the red dots. They just do.

Over time, you'd have sorted out all the icky buttons by marking them, leaving only those buttons that yielded the tasty stuff when pushed. This would be a pretty good system unless…

- There were more than a few buttons. What if there were millions of buttons, instead of just a few hundred? It would take a LONG time to try and mark them all. And if the number of buttons was infinite, you'd never be able to get it done.

- People weren't inclined to try ALL the buttons. It's likely that after a sufficient number of buttons had been marked, people would seek to avoid getting any stinky foot mush by sticking to the part of Vending Machine World that's mapped and not venturing into uncharted territory.

- Not everyone had the same sense of taste. What if what some people considered red-dot worthy wasn't to others? What if some people actually liked stinky foot mush? If newbies were simply taught not to push the red buttons, they would never have a chance to find out.

- The content behind the buttons changed. If the buttons were marked and never pushed again, how would one ever know?

- The system was not as simple as it was presumed to be. What if buttons could be pushed in combination, yielding different results, while society assumed that only one button could be pushed at a time?

- And finally, this would be a good system if your goal were simply to avoid the icky stuff. If you actually wanted to find the best of the best, however, this system of elimination of what is unwanted would be highly inefficient, especially when coupled with the idea that there are more than a *few* buttons.

We've been living in a society that's based on eliminating what's unwanted: one that assumes that we all want the same things (same sense of taste); one that teaches new generations what to avoid (never pushing those buttons again to see if anything different squirts out); one that is based on the assumption that someone else's observation about how the system works, made years ago, is how it actually is now; a system that's geared towards avoiding stuff we don't want, instead of towards finding the tastiest morsels possible.

Now, imagine that one of the designers of Vending Machine World came along and gave you a User Manual – a technical guide to how the vending machines work and how to find what you're actually looking for. A handbook full of hidden buttons, hacks and descriptions of delicious foodstuffs you hadn't even heard of. Would you read the book? Would you actually apply it? Of course, if asked this question, just about everyone would say yes. And yet, in the 'real' world, most people, when faced with this exact same scenario – the chance to apply a totally different method to getting what they actually want – will scoff at it, run away from it and possibly even forbid others from reading it.

I refer to people like that as living in the 'Old World' paradigm or thinking 'Old World Thoughts'. This isn't a judgement, just a differentiation. There's actually great value in that paradigm (more on that later), but we are now living in a time when more and more people are opening themselves up to the 'New World' paradigm, where they can access 'New World Thoughts'.

The Old World is all about avoiding pain (avoiding the red buttons), staying safe (don't stray from the mapped areas, you might encounter stinky feet mush!), limitation (avoid the red buttons and teach others to do the same) and conformity (we all have the same taste).

The main theme of the Old World is pain minimization.

The New World is all about seeking pleasure (finding the buttons that yield the really tasty stuff), adventure (push all the buttons! See what happens! Charge into unchartered territory!), expansion (question observations, gather new data, draw your own conclusions) and individuality (you have the right to like stinky foot mush even if I don't).

The main theme of the New World is pleasure maximization.

Of course, this New World isn't really new. It's the world we could've been living in all along. So, why haven't we? Why did we forget how it really works? Who took all the labels off the vending machines and hid the user manual?

There's value in the fog

Consider that reality is like a game: the best, most awesome, most advanced, most kick-ass, full-immersion virtual reality game EVER. Go ahead and geek out a little, if you need to. I won't judge. When you play this game, you create an avatar (a wee human, for example) that can experience this video game reality as 'real', with feelings and stress and love and pain.

Now consider that, while playing this game, you have the chance to explore different aspects of your personality, of who you are, by placing yourself in different scenarios. We've all done this; we've all imagined how we'd react in hypothetical situations. How many times have you seen a report on the news and declared confidently, 'Well, if that happened to *me*, I would've been way cooler about it than that idiot was.' But how can anyone ever really *know* how they'd react unless they've actually lived that experience? How can you know how it would feel if your boyfriend (or girlfriend) cheated on you unless you've gone through that? You might like to think that you'd automatically leave or forgive him (depending on which one of those appeals more to you), but because nothing is ever black and white, your decisions would depend on a whole host of factors. How long you have been together, for example? Was it a fling or an affair? Do you love him? Do you want to make the relationship work or were you actually ready to leave anyway? Does the fact that he cheated make you feel insecure about yourself? And, most importantly, does he have a six-pack? (If yes, send pics please.)

You can pretend that you know exactly how you'd react, if something like that happened to you. But the truth is, you don't. You can't even imagine all the different combinations of parameters involved, or how you'd feel about any given one. In order to truly know how you'd feel about it, you'd have to *live* it.

Enter the game. By placing yourself in different scenarios, in a way that feels real to you (because how can you fully experience something if you don't think it's real? There's a difference between watching a movie of someone being kissed and actually being kissed), you can truly know how you'd react in any given situation. You can know yourself more fully.

Now, imagine that you're able to create more than one avatar, giving you the ability to experience yourself from any angle, as a serf in 14th-century England, as a Viking warrior(ess?), as Cleopatra or Antony, as a surfer dude in California, as a stockbroker on Wall Street in the 1980s, etc. How would YOU react in any one of these situations? Well, live it in the game and wonder no more!

Of course, this is a game that never ends. Every experience you have gives birth to a new desire. What if the scenario had been only slightly different? What if this time round, you played the game as a man instead of a woman? What if you lived it in a different country? What if this time you were rich?

This is, essentially, what we are doing – WE are creating lots and lots of avatars, all with their own perspective, their own consciousness, at many different levels of the game, who enter the illusion of reality in order for US to experience OURSELVES fully from every angle.

The 'fog' we enter, the one that causes us to forget who we really are, as well as the fact that we are playing a game, is what creates this illusion. Without it, we couldn't experience any situation as real. It's not the same if you *know* it's a game. An actor in a play may feel some of the drama he's experiencing, but nowhere near as fully as if he doesn't realize that it's just a play.

Waking up

Knowing it's a game, however, doesn't *end* the game. It merely changes it. While there's great value in the fog, there's also great value in waking up from that fog: it offers up a whole new set of experiences. When you know who you really are, when you know your power to control your virtual reality world, it's like playing a whole new game. It's a whole New World.

I like to describe the process of waking up like this:

Imagine that you're a world-class tennis player, only you have amnesia, and you don't remember that you know how to play or even what tennis is. You find yourself on a tennis court and suddenly yellow, fuzzy balls come shooting out at you. Some of them even hit you. You feel fear and panic, wondering what the hell is going on. You might stomp your feet and demand that whoever is lobbing those balls at you should stop. And maybe be sent to prison. Hell, let's just outlaw tennis balls while we're at it. That'll fix it. Only, that doesn't work. The balls keep coming, keep hitting you, making you angrier and angrier.

Finally, in a rage, unable to take another second of this crap, you pick up a nearby tennis racket and wildly swing it about. At some point, you connect with an incoming tennis ball and it flies off into the distance. 'Huh,' you wonder. 'What just happened?' You swing some more and hit another tennis ball. You suddenly realize that you're not powerless, that you have the ability to defend yourself. As your pent-up rage comes flying out, you really let those tennis balls have it, whacking them into the distance as hard as you can. This feels good!

After a while, you get a bit tired of angrily smacking at the incoming obstacles, so you begin to play a little. Can you control which direction a ball goes when you hit it? Why, yes, you can! Can you control the distance? Can you put a spin on it and make it fly off in a curve? How accurate is your aim? As your muscle memory takes over, you begin to feel the power and skill you have – that of a world-class tennis player. Your mastery becomes apparent. You no longer mind having tennis balls lobbed at you, in fact, you welcome them. And you don't want the easy ones, either! 'Bring it on,' you yell, happily, enjoying the challenge. The game that used to terrify you now thrills you.

That's what it's like to wake up from the fog. A world that once seemed random begins to make sense. An environment that once seemed mean and unfair now becomes a joyful challenge. Obstacles that once seemed painful are now a welcome part of the game.

You are like that world-class tennis player. You are a master creator; you just don't know it yet – or any more. You're not here to be taught a lesson or to pay your dues or to prove yourself worthy. If you weren't worthy, you wouldn't even be in the game (because it's YOUR game! It's all for YOU!). You're here to experience and to play. And while the obstacles coming at you in the fog can be scary, they don't have to be. They can actually be part of the joy. It's all a matter of remembering who you really are.

There is value in forgetting, but there's even more value (and more fun) in remembering. And while that wasn't possible for most of humanity until now, at this point in our human history, we are experiencing a mass awakening. And yes, that includes you.

If you're reading this book, you're coming out of the fog. You're starting to remember. You're ready to cross the threshold, where you go from the Old World with its focus on pain minimization into the New World, with its focus on pleasure maximization.

Playing the game consciously

You see, when I mentioned earlier that each experience spawned a new desire ('What if I lived that life as a woman this time?'), it may have seemed as though I was saying that each experience spawns a whole new life, a new avatar. And while this is certainly true, this spawning process also takes place from moment to moment.

Each experience you have creates a new desire, which you can then choose to experience, right here, right now. If you eat some chocolate ice cream, you're going to have a reaction to that experience: you'll either like it or not. This will cause you either to want more chocolate ice cream, possibly with sprinkles this time, to try a different flavour, maybe strawberry, or never to eat ice cream again. Even if you hated the ice cream, the experience will give you information about what you don't like and what you want instead (something less sweet, less cold, less chocolaty, etc.).

Even an unwanted experience gives you more information about what you want or, in other words, spawns a new desire.

In fact, this is how new desires are created – you have an experience, and by its very nature, it causes you to want something. Even when you like something and just want more of it, it leads to an evolution of that thing. For example, if you love driving fast, you're not going to drive at the same fast speed down the same stretch of highway. You're going to push that speed (which changes or evolves the experience), and find new and different roads to drive on (which also changes or evolves the experience). You're going to be driven (see what I did there?) to keep making the experience of driving fast bigger, better or more intense.

This is the real-time version of 'What if I did it differently this time?' You don't have to die first and come back as a new avatar (this isn't actually how it happens, but that subject is way beyond the scope of this book). You can live that new experience right now.

This is also why nothing is predetermined (don't think I didn't know that you were wondering about that). Your birth, the situation that you're born into, is just a starting point. From then on, you get to make new decisions on where to take your life in *each and every moment*. In fact, the game depends on your ability to experience *any* desire you create. Each experience begets a new desire which, when lived, is a new experience, which begets a new desire and so on.

When we wake up and begin to play the game consciously, we can choose to live those new desires at will, instead of just hoping they'll someday come true.

The problem arises when we choose *not* to live our desire, but instead, choose to live the experience that creates that desire over and over again. A new desire is created each time we do, but if we don't move towards it, if we don't go with it, it's like hitting the replay button on an old experience. You drive that same stretch of road at the exact same speed every freaking day. *Oh joy* (sarcasm alert!).

That's when the game sends us a message because this sitting in idle isn't at all what the game is about. We don't want to just sit there treading water. It's no fun to run on a hamster wheel and never get anywhere. If you were truly playing a video game and your character was just running in place, it would get pretty boring pretty fast.

The game's built-in feedback system

And this is exactly how the game gets our attention. Boredom is the feeling we get when we sit idle, when we live the same experience over and over again, without making a change. New desires have been spawned, even if it's just 'I don't want this any more', but aren't being chosen. Boredom is both the antithesis and mother of evolution and innovation. It's the antithesis because when you're on repeat mode, you're not innovating or evolving. It's the mother because when you get bored enough, you'll find it so excruciating that you won't be able to help but make a change.

Haven't you ever had the experience of being some place you didn't want to be? Maybe it wasn't even bad, but just some place, well, boring, like a class or a job. Didn't the boredom get bigger and bigger until you just wanted to rip your hair out? Didn't you look for any way to distract or entertain yourself so you wouldn't have to experience the boredom any more? Didn't you get to the point where you just couldn't wait to get out of there?

When you're sitting idle in the game, you get bored. If you continue to sit idle, you'll get even more bored. In fact, the boredom will build until it turns into frustration and anger. The time will come when you won't be able to take it any more and you'll do something about it. You'll make some kind of change. You cannot sit idle forever, because that's not what you came here to do.

Think of it this way: imagine that your avatar is bouncing around in their own little reality. They run around having experiences, creating new desires and then living them, which creates new desires and so on. Let's say that for every experience they have, they get an 'experience point'. The more experience points they accumulate, the more 'life' they have and the better they feel. Think of it as a bar at the bottom of the screen that grows with each experience.

Now imagine that when your character sits idle for a time, the experience points start to decrease. When an experience creates a new desire, that desire floats in front of your avatar like a little coin, ready to be plucked out of the air. If your avatar plucks the coin, one experience point is gained and the character goes on to experience that new desire. If the coin goes to waste, if it's just left there to rot, an experience point is lost. You gain points if you pick up the coin and lose points when you don't.

When your character's 'life' starts to go down, they start to not feel so good. Instead of the vitality they experience when the experience bar is at full force, they start to feel kind of weak and sickly. The lower the point score, the worse the character feels.

Let's say that your avatar falls into a deep pit, where she just runs back and forth. This experience causes her to want out of the pit. A new desire coin is created and floats in front of her. If, however, she doesn't pick up the desire coin, but instead just keeps running back and forth, her experience points will decrease. Each time she has the experience of running back and forth, a new desire coin is released. Each time she doesn't pick that one up, letting it rot, her score goes down and she starts to feel worse.

Eventually, if the avatar just keeps running back and forth, the pain of sitting idle, of having such a low experience score, will become too much and she'll pick up one of the coins and move on.

Believe it or not, you have that exact same feedback system. But instead of experience points (how cool would that be??), you have something else. You have your emotions.

Emotion alert!

Your emotions, how you feel, are your indicator of whether you're going with your newly created desires or not. The longer you go without picking up those desire coins, the longer you keep replaying the same experience over and over again, the worse you'll feel. The more you go with your newly created desires, the better you'll feel.

That's right, your feelings aren't actually useless annoyances that mess up your life. They're an integral part of the reality-creation mechanism.

Now, at this point, you're probably wondering if all of this doesn't seem like we're being 'rewarded' for picking up coins and 'punished' for sitting idle. Well, that might be true, if you were playing someone else's game. But you're not. This is YOUR game. You get to choose your experiences, which create your desires, and you get to choose your reaction – whether or not to pick up the coins. So, when you pick up those desire coins, you are going exactly where you want to go. A desire is something YOU want, not something someone else wants. You're not being rewarded or punished for your reactions, so much as being told whether what you're currently doing is what you really want to be doing.

So, when you are doing what you want to do, when you are going where you want to go, you feel good. When you're not doing what you want to do, for whatever reason, you don't feel so good. When you eat the food you want to eat, it tastes good. When you eat the food you don't want to eat, it tastes bad. That process doesn't include punishment or reward. It's just a feedback mechanism. Do you complain that eating Styrofoam tastes bad, or do you use the information that it tastes bad to make a better tasting choice? Do you feel that it's unfair that drain cleaner doesn't smell yummy, or do you consider it kind of logical and even *helpful*?

Your emotional feedback system is exactly the same. When you are subjecting yourself to an experience that doesn't serve you – something you have lived before and therefore no longer represents a wanted desire – isn't it actually helpful to know that you're doing that? Isn't it logical that doing the same thing over and over again is boring, and the problem isn't that you're feeling bored but rather that you're stuck in idle? The only reason you might consider that feedback mechanism to be a bad thing is if you think, for some reason, that it will be impossible for you to pick up that next desire coin. But in that case, the problem isn't with the game design, or the feedback mechanism, it's with the idea that you *can't* pick up the coin. Because you always can...

You can always realize that next desire. You can always get what you want. In fact, the game depends on it. Without you picking up that desire coin and experiencing that new desire, no new coins can be created and no new experiences can be had. I don't know about you, but a game consisting of a character just running back and forth in a pit doesn't sound like fun to me. The question then becomes, how do we pick up those desire coins and why the hell would we ever choose not to?

Chapter 3

How the Game Works

Why don't we always just pick up those desire coins? In order to answer that, we have to take a look at how the mechanics of the game actually work. You've probably realized by now that by 'the game', I mean reality. When you play the game, you create your reality. When you play the game consciously, meaning that you know you're playing the game, you create your reality deliberately.

I'm totally aware that a lot has been written about reality creation in the last few years, much of it confusing, inaccurate, downright misleading and, let's face it, just total bullshit. It's left a lot of people with a bad taste in their mouths regarding the concept of taking full responsibility for and control of their lives. This is a shame because, when you actually understand this mechanical process, all the changes you've wanted to make, with the various techniques you've read about, actually start to happen.

Here's what creating your reality is NOT:

- Thinking positively and then expecting your life to change magically.

- Looking at all the bad crap that's happened to you and then blaming yourself for it, as in 'you did this to yourself!'

- Sending mind waves to that hottie in your office so they come over and hit on you (if only, eh?).

- Hating yourself and trying to change it by chanting, 'I love myself. I love myself. I love myself' (that's just annoying).

- Anti-religious (reality creation actually blends well with the core truths of most faiths).

- Visualization or vision boards (visualization IS a good tool to use and we'll talk about it later, but simply visualizing on its own doesn't make things happen).

- Watching and censoring everything you and those around you say (DO NOT become THAT person; you know, the one who tells everyone they can't say 'want' or anything that sounds even remotely negative. And yes, cursing is totally fucking allowed. In my book, it's even encouraged... See what I did there?).

- Watching and censoring everything you think and then beating yourself up for your bad, bad thoughts (no self-flagellation required. Extra points if you giggled like a 13-year-old at the word 'flagellation').

- A way to control others (you may be worried about or hoping for this power – either way, no deal).

- Magic (although it will, at times, totally seem like it).

- Just about getting a good parking spot (yep, that IS pretty cool and useful but, honestly, this is about changing your whole life AND getting good parking spots. One does not need to cancel out the other).

- A freaking *secret* (no one is keeping this from you deliberately. You've had the power all along, Dorothy. It's just that, by design, you weren't quite able to remember it while deeply steeped in the fog).

If you've tried some, or all of that stuff, in the past only to have it not work for you, you'll hopefully be relieved right about now. Deliberately creating your reality is not about chanting affirmations, feeling guilty or picturing a car and then having it magically appear. In order to understand what it actually *is*, however, we have to go down the rabbit hole just a little further.

Everything is energy

Let's start with the basics: everything is energy. Everything. At this point in our technological development, that shouldn't be too hard for people to accept, especially when you consider the advancements we've made in quantum physics. We're all just a bunch of quantum particles and/or waves bumping around. Our brain is, among other things, a translator, allowing us to perceive the world around us in a physical or semi-physical way. So we can touch the chair, smell the coffee, taste the chocolate, see the ocean and hear the birds singing.

It is not our eyes that 'see'. Our eyes simply receive light waves in a certain frequency range. It's actually our brain that translates those light waves into something we can perceive as an image. The same thing happens when we touch something with our fingertips. We simply perceive energy, which our brain then interprets for us, so we can experience it. Keep in mind that when you dream, you can feel as though you are actually experiencing something physically, while you're really just lying in bed doing nothing. That's your brain in action.

Everything is energy and it's all vibrating at different frequencies. Our brain can translate some of these frequencies into something we can experience physically.

Consider this: when you download an mp3 file onto your computer, it's nothing but a data file. Really, it's just a bunch of zeroes and ones strung together in a certain sequence. Your computer can interpret those zeroes and ones and then play them back as music, which you can perceive with your ears. Your brain is like that computer. (Remember this metaphor; we'll be coming back to it in just a moment.)

The zeroes and ones that make up the mp3 aren't 'physical'. They can be transmitted via a physical medium, like a CD, but they can also be streamed through the air via a wireless signal. If you tried to show and explain this concept to someone from a couple of hundred years ago, they'd think it was magic (or probably the devil. People back then really, really had a hard-on for the devil). But for us, it's something we've come to accept fully as part of our reality. Physical stuff can exist in a non-physical state. Just because we can't perceive something with our five physical senses doesn't mean it's not there. Information is being streamed at us constantly. All you have to do is switch on your smart phone and you'll have all the proof you need.

So, if you wirelessly download a song, it's in a non-physical state. You chose the song by using your phone or computer to communicate with a non-physical website, and translating it into something you could interpret and interact with. The song comes to you in an energetic from and is then brought into the physical via a device such as an mp3 player. It's only perceivable as physical once you hear it with your ears. You could also print out the album cover, making a physical representation of something that only existed as data up to that point, or even create a 3D model of the band using your 3D printer. (I'm printing out a full-sized version of Hugh Jackman in his Wolverine costume as we speak.) Thanks to advancements in technology, it's easier than ever to understand how we can interact with non-physical energy, and how something non-physical can become solid and touchable. We do it every day.

Downloading reality

This concept of non-physical energy extends far beyond radio and TV signals, microwaves and what I'm sure are *totally* legal downloads of songs, movies and games. Because the book you're now holding (or the device you're reading it on), the chair you're comfortably sitting in, the clothes you're wearing, the car in your driveway, the hottie sitting next to you on the train while you try to think of something clever to say, even YOU, are all made of energy.

You see, playing the mp3 and listening to it doesn't suddenly change the nature of the data; it doesn't change the mp3. It's *still* just zeroes and ones. All that's changed is our perception of the file. Instead of interacting with the file (like downloading it, renaming it, filing it in the right folder), we are now *experiencing* it (listening to it, dancing to it, looking around to make sure no one's watching and then trying out our new, sexy, butt-jiggling moves…).

The act of hitting the play button allows us to experience the song in a physical way. We are, essentially, doing the same with our reality. That chair, the clothes and the hottie are all physical AND non-physical at the same time. We are interacting with non-physical energy, choosing what to download, and then hitting the play button, thereby allowing ourselves to experience it with our physical senses. And Badabing! Badaboom! You've got yourself a heap of physical reality, all made of cosmic zeroes and ones.

This selection of something to download and hitting the play button is what many people want to call the 'process of *creating* your reality'. And up until this point of the book, I have been too. But that's actually not technically accurate.

You see, when you download and play the mp3, you're not creating it. It's already created. It's the same for all of your manifestations – by the time you experience them, they already exist. The desire coin (*see page 25*) is created as soon as you are having an experience. When the desire is created, it exists in non-physical form. The process of perceiving that desire (experiencing it), is what 'brings it into' the physical.

So, when we are talking about manifesting the reality that we want, we're not talking about creating it. The creation of what we want happened as soon as we had the experience that made us want it. What we really want to focus on is the *receiving* part. That's why I didn't call this book 'Deliberate Creating'.

Now, the process of receiving also happens automatically. You know how to receive your reality. In fact, you're a master at it. If you doubt that, look around you. Are there any gaps in your reality? Is there a lack of continuity? Are there dinosaurs running around, or do you sometimes turn around to find a blank space, because you forgot to order and receive that part of the room? Unless you're reading this from a padded cell, I'm going to take a strong guess that the answer is no. You are way better at this shit than you've been giving yourself credit for.

The problem is not with the process of creation or receiving. The problem is with WHAT you are receiving. Your world isn't filled with random stuff. Everything that's in it is there for a reason. And no, it's not to teach you a lesson, or to taunt you or to punish you. It's there because you chose to download it. Or rather, you were told to download it, shown how to download it, and even manipulated and coerced into downloading it. In fact, you were given entire playlists at birth and told they were the best playlists in the world ('No need to go looking for something different, ya hear?')

What you download is, however, a choice. Can it still be considered a choice if you don't know it's a choice, if you're still in the fog? Yes. The fog was a choice, too. However, I'm not here to teach you to choose unconsciously. You're already doing that. I'm here to make you conscious and aware of the choosing and downloading process, so you can experience the reality you want. I'm here to help you change your old playlists. I'm here to teach you about *Deliberate Receiving*.

Downloading deliberately

Your smart phone is a pretty nifty piece of technology. You can interact with all the data on the Internet, search for what you want and find it easily, pay for if need be, download it and use it to experience that media. You can read text, watch movies, listen to music and play games. You can make voice and video calls, get text messages, and sext messages (sexy text messages, or so I hear, *ahem*). You can make notes of things you want to remember, take pictures and even make videos. In short, it's an interface that you can use to interact with non-physical reality, bring it into the physical and experience it.

Your brain is like your smart phone, only way, way cooler. It also has access to the Universal Internet (no modem or provider required!) with all its infinite information. It can search for specific data, download it and then play it back for you in holographic detail. It also automates much of this process, and sets filters based on past searches, but we'll get into that in much more depth in Chapter 5. Your brain is the computer that allows you to interact with non-physical reality, download what you want and experience it in the physical.

The holographic room

Here's how receiving your reality actually works. Imagine yourself in a big, white room. It's filled with nothing but white screens. It's a holographic projection room, like the holodeck on *Star Trek*. Only, instead of a computer or laser projecting a series of images into the room, YOU are the projector. You are a transmitter of energy, emanating frequencies outwards that bounce off the cosmic mirror and are reflected back as your reality. Pretty cool, right?

This is where most people already go astray, because it sounds a bit like 'think of money, get money'. It's also why a lot of people who get into this work think it's all about blame, i.e. 'If you hadn't focused on poverty then you wouldn't be poor.' I'm happy to tell you that this is, once again, a bunch of bullshit. Unlike our holographic technology, which is still in its infancy, the Universal hologram doesn't just reflect back an image. It reflects back a representation of the frequency you emitted. Don't worry; I'll explain this further, because it's a really important point.

Your manifestations (what you experience) are not a match to your thoughts, but to the *vibrations* you emitted. This is why simply thinking of money doesn't get you money, and why thinking of poverty doesn't keep you poor. That's a gross oversimplification of the process and one that probably never sat quite right with you. Good. In the next chapter we'll get into how to tell what your vibration is, but for now just understand that **everything in your reality is a reflection of your *vibration***. Everything.

This applies even to other people. That doesn't mean that other people don't exist. They do. But you are not ever going to experience ALL of them, every single aspect of them. You can only see those parts of them that match your vibration. Have you ever had the experience of seeing someone in a different environment than the one in which you usually interact with them? Maybe you've gone to pick your spouse up at work and realized they're a lot funnier with their co-workers than they are around you. Or, perhaps you've seen a completely different side of your child while watching him playing with his friends. You may have even noticed that you act quite differently depending on whom you're with.

People are a lot more multifaceted than we give them credit for. You can't see all of someone else's facets. You'll only ever see those facets that match the vibration you're projecting. This is why yelling at someone to change or pleading with them or even threatening them doesn't work. They can only ever show you what matches your vibration. They can only ever mirror back your own energy. Trying to change the other person using action or words is like going up to a bathroom mirror and yelling, 'Smile goddammit! I will stand here until you smile, and I will only smile back once you do.' You're not only going to be standing there for a long time, you'll also look totally insane while doing so.

If you want to change your reality, *anything* in your reality, you have to change what's being reflected; you have to change your vibration. The rest of this book will show you exactly how to do just that.

Where's the proof?

Before we go any further, I'd like to address one of the most frequent questions I get asked: Can I prove to you that this is real and that it actually works this way? Well, if I'm going to be honest, and I always am (honestly!)... No. I can't prove anything to you. I can't even prove to you that the sky is blue. Even if I show you scientific data that tells you the sky is there and the light bouncing off our atmosphere causes you to see it as blue, what forces you to believe that the blue I'm talking about is the same as the blue you're seeing? Nothing, that's what. You can't force someone to believe anything. You can manipulate them into pretending they agree with you but, in the end, everyone gets to choose what they actually believe. I may be able to throw enough 'evidence' at you to convince you, but how much evidence is needed to accomplish that is still up to you. You have to accept it as being 'enough'. You have to decide to be convinced.

What you believe is a choice. And because it's a choice, I cannot ever prove anything to you beyond a shadow of a doubt, as long as you choose to have doubts. All I can do is make my case, give you the explanations and metaphors that allow your brain to understand these processes easily, show you examples of people who have successfully applied them and leave it up to you.

I do, however, want to give you some advice. I'm sharing some concepts with you in this book that may be drastically different from what you were taught about how reality works. Choose to accept these concepts and metaphors as real, just for a little while. Choose just to go with it, give it a try, suspend the old way of doing things (that never worked anyway!), and give yourself over to this process. Don't half-ass this, really go for it. See it as a game. Choose to act as if your reality really was a holographic mirror of your vibration (you don't have to believe that it *literally* is, but if you apply this premise even as a metaphor, you'll get real results). There is no real risk involved, except that your life will drastically change for the better.

Which brings me to my second piece of advice: be *willing* to accept change. So many people start this work, only to freak out when stuff actually begins to happen (yes, this crap actually works!). We'll cover how to avoid these freak-outs in Chapter 12, but for now, be open to the idea of your life actually morphing into something different. If you download a different playlist, don't be surprised when the music you hear changes.

There's no judgement

I'd also like to point out another, rather huge, concept: **it is a mechanical process**. There is no middleman involved, deciding *if you deserve* the holographic reflection you've chosen. You are not being punished with 'bad' holograms (as in, you projected one thing but got something else). And you're not being taught any lessons.

How would you feel if you went to Amazon and ordered a book, only to be sent something completely different? Perhaps you ordered a funny romance novel, but received a calculus textbook, with a note from Amazon telling you that you don't get to have fun because you haven't yet paid your dues, because Amazon hates you, or because people like you (insert family name, gender, cultural background, certain physical attributes, personality traits, geography, etc.) can't have nice things. Chances are you'd feel like Amazon had lost their goddamned mind. Very few of you would just sit there and go, 'Oh well, I guess I'd better learn to love calculus' or, even worse, come up with all kinds of justifications for why Amazon was probably right to do what they did.

But that's what people do in their realities every day. They get something they don't want and then make up reasons for why that's OK. We'll be taking a look at a lot of these specific reasons throughout the book, but they all have one thing in common: they all assume that there's judgement involved. Someone or something decided to intervene and give you something you don't want. Someone or something has more power over your reality than you do. It doesn't matter what you order, Amazon and iTunes and eBay decide what you get.

Only, that's just not how it works, and thinking that it is will keep you stuck in a reality filled with unwanted crap seemingly foisted upon you by some outside force. Because as long as you assign the responsibility for what you're receiving to someone outside yourself, even if that's not true, you can never deliberately choose to receive what you actually want. You'll be asking someone else for permission to pick up your desire coins. And because no one else can actually give you that permission (it's YOUR game!), you'll never get it, causing all your coins to rot and your desires to go un-experienced.

This is why the downloading metaphor is so perfect. You choose to order something and you get it. No big whoop. No judgement involved. The idea of needing to deserve it, being a good enough person, or needing to get other people's agreement doesn't even enter into the equation. If you don't get what you wanted, you don't automatically assume that it's *your fault*, that you simply weren't good enough. You never assume that you *can't* get what you ordered. You figure something in the process went wrong. And if you knew that Amazon didn't make mistakes, that you ALWAYS received what you ordered, you'd go back and check your receipt. You'd call Amazon to see if you could figure out where it all went wrong. You wouldn't just sit there and freaking accept that you must now foster a love of calculus.

This metaphor also allows us to introduce another concept: **size doesn't matter**. No, I'm not talking about *that* (admit it; you totally went there). I'm talking about the size of your manifestation. It's all just data, all just zeroes and ones. It's no more difficult for you to download a movie than a single song. And because it's all just data, it's also no more difficult to manifest a mansion than a parking space.

Chapter 4

Focus, Frequency and Feelings

So, if this truly is a simple mechanical process (and it is), and all you have to do is download what you want, then why isn't your life filled with mansions and movie stars? Why aren't you king or queen of the world? Why is Brad Pitt refusing to answer your fan mail? Where is it all going wrong? Let's take a look at how the manifesting process actually works, *how* you place your order and how you *receive* your reality.

When you order something off the Internet, you first have to go to the right website. You can't go to a website that sells curtains to buy a dress (unless you're Scarlett O'Hara, in which case, knock yourself out). You then have to search for what you want, choose it and receive it. If it's an electronic item, you can download it immediately. If it's a physical item that has to be shipped, you'll have to wait a little while.

But the process is always the same:

1. Go to the correct place to find what you're looking for.

2. Search for it.

3. Select it.

4. And then receive it.

Easy-peasy, right?

Well, if it really is that easy, then why don't we constantly receive only what we want, instead of being surrounded by the equivalent of piles and piles of stinky foot mush? It turns out we tend to introduce a few bugs into the system inadvertently.

There are two different points in this process during which you can sabotage a successful outcome – while *selecting and ordering* the item and while *receiving* it.

Ordering and receiving

The 'ordering' process refers to what you are choosing to download; it's the placing of the order. In the holographic room (*see page 36*), this is the emitting of the energy (the frequency you send out, which bounces off the cosmic mirror and gets reflected back to you). If you don't pay attention to what you are choosing, your lovely brain will default to choices you've made in the past – your order history. It's impossible to stop choosing altogether, by the way, as that would cause your entire reality to fall apart and disintegrate, which would be sort of disorienting to say the least and, really, kind of a bummer. Who wants to sit in an empty room? Remember that if you don't choose to realize a newly spawned desire, you're automatically choosing to have the same experience again. In either case, you're still always choosing. But you can choose deliberately or by default. You can experience deliberately or by default. I suggest you do both deliberately, but that's just me.

We'll be looking at precisely how you can interfere with the ordering process in just a moment.

You can also interfere with the delivery of your order during the receiving process – the experiencing of it (hitting play and listening to the song). How you choose to experience something determines what desires are created from it, which determines your next experience. If you choose to see something as positive, your desire may be for that same experience to intensify. If you choose to see something as horrible, your desire will be for something completely different.

So, how you choose to perceive the hologram actually changes the hologram. Don't you worry, I'll be breaking this down into much more detail later in this chapter. But first, we have to talk about how you're actually doing the choosing.

Choosing your vibration (what you're sending out)

How, exactly, do we choose what to order? How do we even know what we're emitting (what we have ordered)? Well, the easiest way to figure out the second one is to look at your hologram – at your reality. What's being mirrored back to you? If your reality is filled with a bunch of stuff you adore, you've got a great vibration. If it's full of a bunch of unwanted crap, you may have some tweaking do to. I'm guessing that you've got at least some unwanted stuff floating around in your world, or you wouldn't be reading this book; you'd just be blissfully happy, probably swimming in a pool filled with chocolate sauce and strawberries and having your every need being tended to by hunky vampires. Or maybe that's just me.

Remember how everything is energy? That means everything is vibrating at a certain frequency. When you focus your attention on something, you activate its frequency. In the video game analogy, if you had your avatar look at an object, say, a tree, it would start to vibrate and glow.

As you activate the frequency of something (a thing, a concept, anything), the Law of Attraction kicks in. Now, I know, you've probably heard of the Law of Attraction, or LOA for short, but, unfortunately, a lot of what you've heard may have been full of – how do I put this delicately? – the main export from the Crap

Factory in Craptown, by way of Bullshit County, in the Land of Misinformation. I can't help that. What I can do is explain to you what the Law of Attraction actually is, what an important part it plays in the process of receiving your reality, and why you should stop rolling your eyes at it (you know who you are).

The Law of Attraction, in a nutshell, states that any frequency that is activated will cause other representations of that frequency to join it.

Oh dear Gawd, what the hell does that mean? Don't worry, I'll explain. When people study the Law of Attraction, this is actually the point that they most frequently get wrong.

Notice that the above definition contains the phrase 'representation of frequency'. When we talk about the frequency of something in this context, we are not actually talking about its *physical* frequency, something one could measure with a physical device. We are talking about the frequency it evokes in the observer. This is a huge and all-important distinction.

When you focus on something, and therefore activate it, you are entering into a type of interaction with that thing. You and it are 'communicating'. No, the luxury car you're looking at isn't going to tell you its life story. But you will notice that focusing on the car will cause you to experience a feeling about it. Anything you choose to focus on will evoke a reaction from you. You can't help it. Once you have an experience of something, once it enters your reality, you'll have a reaction to it. You'll have an opinion about it, if you will. This opinion will be based on the emotion you felt as you had the experience.

Remember that your emotions are your vibrational feedback system, letting you know if you're going for what you want (realizing your desires) or not (choosing to sit idle and have the same experiences over and over).

By focusing on an object or idea, the observer's vibration will become a match to what that object or idea represents *to the observer*, NOT the frequency of the object itself. You see, when you look at a chocolate ice-cream cone, it will not affect you in the same way as another person looking at that same chocolate ice-cream cone. You may love chocolate, for example, while they prefer vanilla. That ice-cream cone will not represent the same experience to each of you, it will not feel exactly the same to each of you, and will therefore not attune you to the same frequency.

To you, in your reality, that ice-cream cone will have a different frequency (will *represent* a different frequency) than it will for someone else in their reality. What frequency something has is relative – to you the observer and what you want. It is your perspective, how you feel about it, what it represents to you and what you want that determines its frequency in your reality. As you focus on the ice cream and think about eating it, you actually begin to vibrate at the frequency *it represents to you*, and you begin to emit or *send* that frequency out into your holographic reality, where it is reflected back to you.

If what you are focusing on feels good to you (positive emotional feedback), then you are emitting a frequency close to what you want (the better you feel, the closer your vibration is to what you want). If what you are focusing on feels bad to you, then you are emitting a frequency far away from what you want (the worse you feel, the farther away your vibration is from what you want).

So, you choose your vibration (what you send out into your holographic room and therefore what shows up in your reality) by choosing what to focus on and paying attention to how it feels. The better something feels to you, the 'higher' your vibration. The worse something feels, the 'lower' your vibration. Using 'higher' and 'lower' to refer to vibration in this way isn't technically accurate as it's all relative, but for the sake of convenience many teachers, including me, refer to a vibration that is more closely aligned with what you want as 'higher', and a vibration that is less aligned with what you want as 'lower'. Therefore, a higher vibration is one that feels better to you, and a lower vibration is one that feels worse to you.

I cannot stress this enough: it's not just what you're focusing on that determines your vibration or what you're choosing to download. It's how you feel about what you focus on as you focus on it. The thing you're focusing on is merely a *representation* of a vibration. Everything is just a representation of vibration. You choose to match the vibration of *what that thing represents to you* by focusing on it.

This is why the idea that you literally get what you think about is fundamentally flawed and leads to so much confusion. You get what matches the vibration you're emitting as you think about something. You can't just focus on money to get money. You have to take a look at what money represents to you and how it feels, and then check on whether or not you're aligned with *that*. Don't worry, I'll be taking you through the process of aligning you with what you want in much greater detail later in this book.

How what you focus on manifests

How, exactly, does the Law of Attraction actually fit into all of this? To answer that, let me introduce you to one of the most important concepts of this book. We're going to look at the mechanics of how non-physical energy becomes physical or, in other words, how stuff actually manifests into your physical reality.

When you focus on something, the frequency that this something represents is activated within you. As you continue to focus on it, it becomes more and more 'active'. The Law of Attraction causes whatever you are activating to 'grow'. It actually draws more and more particles to you that match the exact frequency you're activating. This is why we say, what you focus on grows. It literally does! And I know that many grammar angels out there are going to say, 'No, it doesn't *literally* grow. If I stare at an apple, it will not get bigger.' And they'd be right, as long as you're talking about the apple's physical frequency, not its representational frequency, that is.

The Law of Attraction is the mechanism by which what you focus on grows, but you have to remember that you're talking about the frequency of what the thing you're focusing on represents. No, the apple will not get bigger as you stare at it, and no, you probably won't get a bunch more apples (although you might). But let's say that you hated apples. They disgust you. Apples represent a frequency to you that feels like disgust. As you look at an apple and feel that disgust, it won't take long for other stuff that matches that frequency, stuff that also feels disgusting (and probably even more disgusting than the apple) to enter your reality.

Let's take a closer look at how this process works – exactly how manifestations come into being.

💥 Progression of a Manifestation 💥

I'm going to use a simplified, theoretical example in order to help make this point clearly. We'll get to the real-world examples, once we've covered all the basics. We're going to choose a target that feels good, but the mechanics of this apply whether what you're focusing on is wanted or unwanted. In other words, all manifestations, both positive and negative, follow this Progression.

Stage 1: You focus on something of your choice

Consider that you're focusing on a big red rose. You have to imagine it because there isn't any rose physically present in your reality but, in your imagination, it looks exquisite and smells divine. It's not hard at all for you to focus on it. As you do, you activate the frequency that the rose represents to you.

Stage 2: You feel an emotion

As you activate the frequency that the rose represents to you, you feel a corresponding emotion. This emotion is your first manifestation. It could not have occurred if you hadn't activated the frequency that triggered it. The emotion is a result of, or a response to, an active frequency. This is your vibrational feedback. Without this feedback, you have no way of knowing what you're actually focusing on. Think of it this way: if you point a laser pointer at the wall, you have no way of knowing exactly where you're pointing until you see the little red dot. You need some kind of feedback to let you know where you're focusing that laser, and you need some kind of feedback to know exactly what it is you're focusing on in terms of receiving your reality.

In the example of the rose, let's say you're feeling love. So, by focusing on the rose, you're actually activating a frequency that feels like love. Since love feels good, you know that you're successfully aligning with something you want. So, you keep going; you keep on focusing on the mental picture of that rose. If something feels off to you, if the emotion you're noticing feels negative, this emotional stage is your first opportunity to adjust your focus until it feels better.

Stage 3: Thoughts, memories and ideas

In the next stage of manifesting, you'll notice more thoughts and memories that feel like love flooding in. You may suddenly recall how your grandmother used to give the best hugs and how she made you feel loved. You may begin to imagine other flowers or images of seemingly unrelated objects or ideas that feel like love to you. As the frequency of what you're focusing on becomes more and more active, as the Law of Attraction causes more and more energy to join in, more representations of that energy will show up. Thoughts, memories and ideas are all manifestations. Notice that thoughts come AFTER emotions in the Progression. It may seem like you think a thought and then have an emotional reaction, but the thoughts you have access to are actually determined by your emotional state (and if you go deeper, your vibration).

If you're not a vibrational match to a thought, such as 'I love myself', for example, you can chant it all day long, but you won't be able to attune to that thought and feel it. You won't be able to activate the vibration of feeling loved. Saying the words and actually activating the frequency you think they represent are two different things. We'll cover why that is in greater detail in Chapter 6, but for now, remember that your thoughts don't determine your vibration; your vibration determines your thoughts. As you activate a frequency, you'll first manifest a corresponding emotion, after which thoughts and memories that match that representational frequency (or the same emotion) will show up.

Stage 4: Synchronicities appear

Synchronicities are smaller physical manifestations that represent a frequency to you but don't necessarily mean anything to anyone else. For example, you might hear a song on the radio that feels like love to you, but the person you're with doesn't see the connection between the song and what you've been focusing on. A lot of people love the synchronicities of numbers, such as seeing 11:11 on their clocks. Someone at the grocery store may make a comment to you, reminding you of something that feels like love. You might see a billboard with a meaningful (to you) message. These small events are easy to miss or dismiss, but they're the first signs of your manifestation becoming physical. Be careful not to dismiss these events as meaningless, as coincidences (no such thing, it's ALL a mirror!), or as nonsense because others in your reality don't agree with you. Representational frequency is a uniquely personal thing.

Stage 5 to infinity: The physical manifestations grow

At this point, something that feels like love will come into your reality, something you almost can't miss. (I say 'almost', because people do still miss manifestations at this stage…) Starting in stage 5, you'll begin to see what most people would call 'real' physical manifestations. You might meet a hot, new romantic partner, for example. These manifestations are obvious enough that others will be able to validate them, although they may not necessarily do so.

It's at this point that most people make a huge mistake and totally mess up their vibration. You see, manifesting is an ongoing Progression, and stage 5 is not the *last* stage. Manifestations continue to grow and evolve. Basically, they get bigger and more obvious.

People often mistake the first larger physical manifestation for 'the one', be it the one job, the one partner, the one and only chance they'll ever get to have what they want. Often, you'll get a manifestation that feels quite a bit like what you want, but doesn't completely match it once you dig a little deeper. This is called a 'precursor', a concept we'll be covering in detail in Chapter 12, but the main point to remember here is that manifestations happen in a Progression. You don't have to settle for the picture of what you want instead of the real thing, you don't have to settle for a house that's pretty on the outside but a horrible mess on the inside, and you don't have to settle for a good-looking guy who's actually a douchebag.

Stage 5 is also where action comes into play. That's right, action is a manifestation. What you say and do HAS TO BE a match to your vibration. I'm going to say this again: You can't actually take action that's not a match to the vibration that you're offering.

When you try to manipulate or change your reality with action that doesn't match the vibration of what you want, you fail to bring about what you want. You're working on a stage-5 manifestation (the result), rather than the cause (the vibration itself). You may have heard the term 'inspired action'. All action is inspired action, because all action is inspired by a vibration, just not necessarily the vibration of what you want.

❧

If you'd like a quick reminder of the Progression of a Manifestation as you're reading through the book, you can find a summary in Appendix III (*see page 245*). *You're so totally welcome.*

The Progression of a Manifestation in action

For example, let's say you want to lose weight. You think that if you exercise, you'll drop pounds, and so you force yourself to do so. You also force yourself to go on a diet. You're not a vibrational match to what you want – being thin, but you're going to try and change your body through action. If you don't become a vibrational match to being thin, you will never lose the weight and/or keep it off. Even if you do manage to force your body to drop some weight, you'll only end up gaining it all back. The torturous action you took was not a match to thinness, but a match to the frustration you feel at not being able to lose weight. If you're frustrated with being fat, this diet and exercise programme may have been a way for you to punish yourself. Losing some weight and gaining it back will be a perfect way to mirror back that frustration to you in an even more obvious way. If you want to do something, but can't seem to force yourself to do it, it's only ever because the frequency of what that action represents to you doesn't actually match the vibration you're emanating.

When we talk about 'inspired action', however, we're usually referring to action inspired from a place of being a match to what we want – meaning, action that will take us closer to that wanted manifestation. This kind of inspired action requires us to become a match to what we want *before* taking action. It's incredibly important to understand that action does not bring about change. You cannot force your physical reality to change by taking action. You can't change the hologram by swiping at it with your hands any more than you can change what your bathroom mirror is reflecting by wiping at it, punching it or pleading with it. You can only ever effect change by altering what's being reflected. So, when you focus on trying to make something happen through action, you're in for a frustrating ride. The key is to change the vibration to one that matches what you want and let the Progression inspire the action that matches that frequency. This type of inspired action is easy, feels good and is incredibly effective (it actually works).

This is also why our willpower fails so often: it wasn't designed to be used in conjunction with action. Most people think their willpower is there to help them change some kind of habit or action to another one, like forcing themselves to start jogging, or quit smoking. Our tool of willpower is actually there to help us make a change in how we focus. Thanks to the Law of Attraction supporting that focus by immediately bringing more manifestations that match what we're focusing on, our willpower doesn't actually have to last very long. Which, incidentally, is why it doesn't.

As long as you continue to match and emanate a frequency, the Progression of a Manifestation that matches it will never end. Not only do the manifestations get bigger and more obvious, they get more *intense* – meaning, they will evoke a stronger and stronger emotional reaction from you.

You can tell by how you feel if you're continuing with the Progression or not. Notice that I didn't say that you had to feel good to continue manifesting. All of these stages will apply equally to the manifestation of unwanted things. So, if you continue to focus on something that feels bad, you'll get more and more evidence of that, too.

Choosing your experience (what you're receiving)

Now that you understand how you choose what to download into your reality, and the basics of how it manifests into the physical, let's take a closer look at how you might be filling your reality with crap you don't want by messing up your vibration while *receiving* your manifestation.

As I explained in stage 5 of the Progression of a Manifestation (physical manifestations), it's easy to misinterpret the manifestations we get. When we decide, for example, that a specific manifestation is the 'final' or perfect representation of what we want, even though focusing on it feels increasingly off, we can actually cause a misalignment in our energy (we stop focusing purely on what we want) and stop the Progression of wanted manifestations. We can also try to make unwanted manifestations (the crap) go away by yelling at it and pushing it away and kicking at it and banishing it. This, however, doesn't work at all. When you focus on what you don't want, you bring more representations of that energy into your reality, just the same as when you focus on what you do want. The process is mechanical. It doesn't care if you want it or not. If you focus on it, you're getting it. When you press the button on a vending machine, you're going to get whatever that button said, whether you *meant* to push it or not.

Your reaction to your manifestations at any stage (stage 2 to infinity) is actually what kicks off the next stage 1 (you focus on something new). Focusing on anything in a way that doesn't match the vibration you've deliberately chosen to hold will kick off a whole new Progression.

Let me give you a few examples to illustrate this concept:

- You're focusing on the rose and it feels good, but you then let the annoying guy in your office get your attention and you focus on that instead. You're now heading down a whole new Progression. You'll be manifesting stuff that feels annoying.

- You were focusing on a rose and you manifested the picture of a rose, but you assumed that this was your one and only manifestation of that frequency and so were disappointed by the fact that it was only a picture. Your disappointment shows you that you are now no longer a match to what the rose represents, and will no longer continue down that Progression. You've started down a new Progression. One of disappointment.

- You were focusing on a rose and you manifested a song that feels like love (the frequency the rose represents to you). But instead of perceiving the song as part of your love Progression, you choose to see it as a reminder of how hopelessly single you are, causing you to sink into sadness and frustration. You have now started a new Progression, one that leads to more desperate singleness (as opposed to awesome singleness) instead of love.

This is why the RECEIVING part of the equation is actually just as important in deliberately getting what you want as the ORDERING part. It's only through the evidence (the emotion, the thoughts and memories, the synchronicities, the stuff, etc.) that you know what you're actually focusing on, allowing you to make adjustments. By looking in the mirror, you're able to see what's being reflected, allowing you to make changes that will then allow the reflection to change. It's your reaction to that reflection that determines what frequency you're going to be emanating next. In this way, your reaction to a manifestation actually sets off your next Progression of a Manifestation, and therefore determines what's going to manifest next in your reality.

What went wrong?

We've now covered the basic mechanics of how reality creation works – how manifestations come into the physical, and how you can control what you manifest into your reality. But, if this is actually how it works (and it is), why, *in the Gawd-forsaken hell*, aren't we all just focusing on what we want? Why aren't we using this mechanical process to create only realities that feel good? What, exactly, are we doing wrong and WHY?

It turns out that we don't just focus on what feels good. In fact, most of us humans (interestingly, we are the only species on Earth that does this) spend more time focusing on crap that doesn't feel good. But why would we do this? I mean, haven't we proven that humans are actually wired to avoid pain and seek pleasure? Isn't the avoidance of pain actually one of our biggest motivating factors?

Yes, we did and, yes, it is. So why, then, are we still in so much pain? Where is the bug in this equation?

Chapter 5

The Anatomy of Resistance

We all want to feel good. This is true for everyone, even the most miserable among us. We, like all beings, are wired to seek pleasure and to avoid pain. So why is it that so many of us are still in so much pain? Unless the game is broken, which it isn't, why would we even include the ability to create so much crap? Why are we so good at filling our holographic realities with so much unwanted stinky foot mush and so bad at filling them with chocolate-filled swimming pools? In order to answer that, we'll delve deeply into how we humans tick, how other humans have taught us to sabotage focusing on and receiving what we actually want and, more importantly, how to change all of that.

We humans will actually willingly and often deliberately focus on something that doesn't feel good, thereby bringing more evidence of that feeling into our realities. We will actually interfere with the frequency of what we want, by attuning ourselves to something that doesn't match, something that *resists* that good -feeling frequency.

Why would we do this? Well, it's not because we're stupid or crazy. It's because we have *resistance*. But what, exactly, is resistance?

Resistance is any perspective that causes us to focus willingly on something that does not feel good by making it seem that the painful option is the best-feeling option we have access to.

Let's get one thing straight. No one wants to suffer. No one wants to be in pain. No living thing will ever *willingly* and *consciously* move away from pleasure and towards pain, not even humans. It may often seem like we're running towards the suffering, but what we're really doing is running away from something even worse. No exceptions.

If you see two options, you will always choose the better-feeling one (according to your perspective). Someone from the outside could easily see a third option that holds a lot less suffering and wonder why you didn't choose that one. They might even try to persuade you to take that third option and then call you an idiot for not choosing it. But what they don't see is that you hold a perspective that filters out that third option, making it completely unavailable to you.

Let's go back to the Amazon analogy of Chapter 3 (*see page 39*). When you search for something on Amazon, you have the ability to filter those search results, meaning you block out many of the potential options in order to narrow down what's left, making it easier to find what you're looking for. This is generally a good thing; it's a mechanism that allows you to find that perfect book or pair of shoes in a lot less time and with much less effort. You don't have to look at *everything* that's available. You don't have to sift manually through the entire inventory of what Amazon sells. You can narrow down the search to clothing, then to shoes, then to black high heels in a certain size. The more filters you set, the fewer results you'll get. If your search criteria are good, you'll be filtering out all the items that you don't want right now, and leaving only what matches what you're looking for.

But what if your search criteria were bad? What about if you forget to clear your search filters from one search to the next? Perhaps your parents searched for something last and their search parameters are still in place. What if you're applying filters to a search for blue shoes, when you're actually looking for black shoes? Well, instead of helping you to find the shoes you want faster and more easily, those filters would actually be getting in your way, blocking out the results you truly want.

If you were unaware that Amazon had this search filter function, you might assume that they didn't have any black shoes for sale, seeing as there weren't any in your search results. You'd settle for some dark blue shoes perhaps, assuming that this was the best you could do. You might even choose a truly ugly pair of shoes, simply because it was the best of the ones that were available, and well, you need shoes.

But the truth is that Amazon does have a search filter function, and you do know about it. When you don't find what you're looking for, you don't assume that what you want isn't available (you know they have black shoes! They freaking have everything). You erase the search filters and start again. You understand that if the results you're seeing don't match what you want, you must simply not be seeing them. So, you change your perspective (you change the filters), until you're successful.

When it comes to manifesting, the Universe also has a search filter function and, just like Amazon, when you don't get the search results you want it is never because what you want isn't available, or isn't available *to you*. It's always due to a filter in place that is blocking out those results. These filters, or limiting perspectives, are also called 'Limiting Beliefs'. Limiting beliefs are a type of resistance.

Hold on, I can hear you asking, why would limiting beliefs even be part of this game? Isn't that a little cruel? If limiting beliefs are all that stand between nirvana and us then what the hell, Universe? Why include them at all? Well, why does Amazon have a search filter function? The answer is, so you can find what you're looking for more quickly and easily! It's actually a useful tool, or at least, it starts off that way.

We choose what to believe (free will)

You may recall that in Chapter 2, I mentioned that you choose what to believe, and you do. You can choose to believe anything you want, choose whatever side of a debate you want to be on and have whatever opinion and preference you want. This is called 'free will', and it's an integral part of the game. After all, the game can't continue if an experience causes you to create a desire that you can't realize. Remember that it's only when we actually engage with our desires and take advantage of the opportunities that present themselves to us that we have a *new* experience (as opposed to simply living the same experiences over and over again), allowing us to spawn a new desire and keep the game going.

Now, in order truly to have free will, you have to have the ability to choose *any* perspective. If someone else has gone in there and limited your options, having judged some of them as unwanted on your behalf (like Amazon deciding that you, in particular, don't get to buy black shoes), then you don't truly have total choice. So, all options, including marrying a douchebag, for example, have to be choosable. This does not mean that you chose to marry your douchebag-ex just to prove that you were free to do so. Free will dictates that choosing him had to be an option (just as everything is an option), but that's not why you actually married him.

You chose to marry a douche because in that moment, at that time, it was the best-feeling option you had access to (or you thought it was). It was the option that actually did feel best to you out of all the options you could see. You didn't knowingly marry a douche (as in 'I know he's a douche and that I'll be deeply unhappy, but I'm marrying him anyway'). In fact, this is probably part of the information that was being filtered out. There was a lot about that situation that you simply couldn't perceive. You may be able to see more now, having changed your filters, but given the search parameters you had in place then, marrying that guy was actually the best-feeling option you had access to.

You made the best choice you could, given the *beliefs* you had at the time. Your beliefs are your search filters. They determine what search results (options) you can perceive.

But what, exactly, is a belief, anyway? And how does it become 'limiting'?

A belief is an automated thought, opinion or reaction.

Every thought, opinion, reaction, decision or perspective you've accepted as 'true', and therefore keep repeating, can be considered a belief. If you've made the decision that you like Bob, for example, and every time you see or hear of or even think of Bob, you do so from the perspective of liking him, it won't take long before your brain will automate the process. So, when you see Bob, you'll automatically have a smile on your face. You'll automatically give him the benefit of the doubt when you hear something negative about him. You invite him to your parties, look for him, interact with him, talk to him in a friendly voice, use friendly body language and eye contact, and attribute positive qualities to him that you may never have seen him demonstrate. You've made your decision about Bob, and you keep applying it to him every time he shows up in your reality.

On the other hand, if you decide that you hate Bob, every time you see or hear of or even think of Bob, you do so from the perspective of hating him. It won't take long before your brain will automate the process. So, when you see Bob, you automatically have a smirk on your face. You automatically believe anything negative you hear about him. You don't invite him to any parties, do your best to avoid him, talk to him in a disinterested or even unfriendly voice, use hostile or cold body language, make little eye contact and attribute negative qualities to him that you may never have seen him demonstrate.

You automatically react according to your beliefs. When you think of Bob, you're not neutral, the way you are about someone you know nothing about and haven't met. You have beliefs about Bob, which run like a program on your computer brain. These programs get executed whenever you encounter the concept of Bob in any way (someone could simply remind you of him, and the program will run just the same as if he's walked into the room).

Once you have your first reaction to something, once you've made a decision about something, you have a thought about it. If you think that thought just a few times, it becomes automated. Think about how quickly any action you take regularly becomes a habit.

Now, they say that it takes 28 days to form a new habit, but the people who say this are usually talking about breaking an old habit and replacing it with a new one (e.g. quit smoking or stop eating junk food), or trying to force themselves to do something they don't really want to do but think they should (e.g. go to the gym when they don't really enjoy it). In fact, when we talk about habits, the 'bad' that precedes it (bad habits) is usually implied. 'I have a habit of…' is almost never followed by something positive, like 'cuddling puppies', but much more likely to be something we want to stop doing. We've elevated the formation of habits to something horrible and difficult in our society. But the actual mechanism of habit formation isn't about forcing ourselves to do something we don't want to do. It's simply about *automation* – the automation of stuff that we do over and over again.

The actual mechanics of forming a habit are easy, simple and effortless. And it doesn't take anywhere near 28 days. In fact, it begins the second you repeat any action, thought or perspective. It's one of your brain's main functions and your brain is very, very good at it. Think about this: if you had to make every decision from scratch, *every single one*, you'd be totally overwhelmed.

If you had to weigh up logically the pros and cons of which coffee to drink, which cup to drink it from, which pen to write with, which undies to wear, which route to take to work, and disregard all the criteria you've used in the past (i.e. you suddenly have no idea which coffee tastes better to you, etc.) you'd be shut down by the most mundane of tasks. Instead, you've built up a database of observations and preferences based on your experiences over time. You've tasted several types of coffee and have chosen the one you like the best. You figure the chances are pretty good that you'll still like that one the best today, and so you choose it automatically. Or, in other words, you have a belief that this one coffee is the best. You don't have to think about it at all. You accept the decision you made in the past as 'true', i.e. to you that coffee really is the best, and so you simply apply this 'truth' to your life. Automating that decision frees your mind up to be able to focus on other things, just like automating all the actions required to drive a car frees you up to fantasize about smacking the guy who's been tailgating you for the last mile and a half in the back of the head... with a frying pan.

You've made your decision about the coffee and the pen and all the rest, and you're working from those old decisions. And for the most part, this system serves you very well. Until it doesn't.

A limiting belief is a belief that once served you, but no longer does.

Let's say that a new brand of coffee has just come out. It blows all the other brands out of the water. You love coffee and pride yourself on drinking only the best. If, however, you insist that the decision you made in the past, that the coffee you're currently drinking *is* the best and *will always be* the best, disregarding the fact that your decision was based on a limited sample (you have not tried EVERY possible coffee in the world and this new brand wasn't available when you made your decision), you won't even be open to trying this new one.

As we live and experience and evolve, we have to be willing to upgrade our beliefs, our perspectives and opinions. We have to be willing to bring in new data and come to new conclusions. This sounds like a no-brainer, right? Well, many of the world's problems are directly attributable to people not being willing to do just that – they're not willing to upgrade their beliefs.

Beliefs gone bad

Let's take a look at some examples of how a well-functioning belief, which makes your life easier, turns into a limiting belief that stands between you and a life filled with mansions and chocolate fountains. (Not one of those little fountains you see at a buffet, either. I'm talking the normal-sized fountain you'd see in a large garden or in the centre of a European town square. Only, filled with chocolate. You know that fountain is going to be in your fantasies now. *You're welcome.*)

Case study: The Earth is flat

Consider that we used to believe that the Earth was flat. This belief seems incredibly limiting to us now. It would keep us from flying planes around the world, the entire shipping industry wouldn't exist, we certainly couldn't have gone into space and there would probably be no Internet shopping. (I'm guessing. There's no way to know this for sure. I like to think that the geeks of the world would still have found a way.) If you thought you could fall off the edge of the world, how far would you travel from home, from the environment you knew to be safe? So clearly, we can consider this to be an outdated, limiting belief.

But there was a time when the belief that the Earth was flat actually served people, never mind that they had it wrong. Consider that thousands of years ago (not during the modern historical time of Columbus when people no longer believed in a flat Earth; that's a total myth), most people's world was very, very small. They had neither the interest nor the means to travel outside of their tribe or village, much less around the globe. Sure, some nomadic tribes moved around quite a bit, but always on land.

Not only did people not have the means to do a large amount of travel, much of the world was still unknown and therefore scary. Who could know what dangers lurked out there beyond the horizon? A flat-Earth theory gave people a justification for staying put, for staying where they felt safe. It justified their fears (because if your fears are justified you're not a coward; the flaw isn't yours).

So, believing the Earth was flat not only served the people of ancient times, it didn't limit them at all. They were never going to be booking any round-the-world tickets. But, at some point, this belief could no longer be applied successfully. The world started to change and humans wanted to explore. If they wanted to travel by sea, they would have to change their belief that the Earth was flat and that they could, potentially, fall off the edge of it. They had to upgrade their belief in order to keep evolving, to do what they wanted to do.

Case study: I'm unworthy

Joey, age five, wants to play. His dad, who's been working all day and is dead tired, is sitting in the living room, drinking a beer and watching the game. He's irritated by something that happened at work and just wants to unwind. Joey, however, doesn't know that. He barges into the room full of joy and energy, and begins to shoot his big, purple toy gun at his dad, challenging him to a duel. He always has a lot of fun playing cops and robbers with his dad, and doesn't see any reason why today might be different. He yells at his 'robber' to 'put 'em up!' giggling and beaming as he brandishes his weapon. Only, instead of jumping up and playing along, his dad loses his temper. The anger he's been holding back at work comes flying out and he screams at Joey to stop bothering him.

Joey runs out of the room, heartbroken. His joy is completely gone. He drops his Nerf gun and sheriff's hat and crawls into his special hiding place under the stairs. What happened? His five-year-old brain can't make any sense of it. He doesn't know that his dad is stressed about work. That's not part of his world and can't enter into his perspective. He has to come to an observation, a conclusion based on the data he has access to. He sees two choices.

First: Life is unpredictable and sometimes really hurtful things just happen. There's no way to know when they will happen and there's nothing he can do about it. In short, Joey can choose to believe in total powerlessness, which feels awful.

Second: He can decide that he must've done something wrong. He's not aware of what it could be but clearly, since his dad yelled at him, he's the one who messed up. Now, while this option doesn't feel great, either, it feels a hell of a lot better than total powerlessness, because at least this way he can do something *about it. He can pay attention and be a good boy and learn to read body language.*

Joey doesn't have enough data to conclude that his dad was being unfair in that moment, that his outburst had nothing to do with his son, but was about something completely different. And if his dad sees Joey's smiling face and quiet yet appeasing manner later that evening as a sign that his son is fine and has 'gotten over it', and therefore never apologizes or explains his anger, Joey will continue to take responsibility for how the adults around him behave. It doesn't take too many incidents like that to create the automated belief that everything that happens around him is his fault.

Then, as a five-year-old, that belief served him. Since Joey could only see two options, he chose the less painful one, the less limiting one. Many severely limiting beliefs are chosen simply to make sense of a seemingly senseless situation. And, at the time of their choosing, they serve the individual in some way. In fact, Joey would've gotten quite a bit of positive feedback that this belief was valid. By checking on his parents' mood before loudly bursting out with his news or asking a question, he could choose the moment at which they were most likely to be open to what he was saying, causing him to have fewer negative experiences.

Now 30 years old, Joey still takes responsibility for how those around him feel. This belief is mirrored back to him in his holographic reality, and he attracts a girlfriend who is highly emotionally charged, or what one might call a 'drama queen'. Being a perfect match to his belief (as all mirrors are), she blames him every time something doesn't go her way. Every time she freaks out, he feels it's his fault and she's only too happy to support this feeling of his. He manifests the same pattern in his job, where his boss picks on him every chance he gets. He never stands up for himself because his belief tells him it's his own damn fault.

This belief that once helped him avoid total powerlessness has now become the ball and chain around his ankle, keeping him from moving into total empowerment and joy.

Most of our older beliefs were not chosen to maximize joy, but to minimize pain. A belief can serve you by simply being less painful than its alternative.

All beliefs are observations

Limiting beliefs aren't 'bad'; they're simply programs that have outlived their purpose. They really are no more sinister than that. Just as you don't want to try and work with software that was designed 20 years ago and never updated (it's slow, has limited functionality and won't let you do what you want to do), you don't want to live your life with old, outdated beliefs.

To some degree, all beliefs are limited (they're all search filters). All of our opinions, decisions, observations and conclusions are based on limited amounts of data. If we look at science throughout history, for example, we believed quite a few things about the human body and how biology worked that turned out to be either total hogwash or only somewhat correct. In either case, we were wrong because our observations were always based on incomplete data. Of course, we totally know everything there is to know NOW, right? Right?

Well, no. We can never know all there is to know. And that's because all there is to know is constantly expanding (just as the Universe is expanding). If a new desire is born every time we have an experience and the evidence that fulfils that desire is created (not yet brought into the physical, not yet necessarily experienced, but created just the same), then we can never run out of experiences to have – there will always be more. In fact, the Universe isn't just expanding, it's expanding exponentially, considering that each experience can and usually will spawn more than one desire.

If the act of experiencing something is simply the discovery of something that already exists, that has already been created, and the very act of experiencing it creates more stuff for us to discover and experience, then we can never run out of stuff to discover and experience. We can never know it all. The data we can perceive will always be incomplete.

So, if it's impossible for us ever to have all the data on any given experience, we will, to some degree, always come to a flawed, incomplete observation. We'll always be at least slightly 'wrong'. Whenever we discover new data, we can and should use it to upgrade our beliefs, to come to new conclusions, and to make new decisions.

The beliefs we form on any given subject will always become obsolete at some point in our evolution. All beliefs are destined to become limiting beliefs. Computer programmers understand this. No piece of hardware or software will last forever. Newer versions are being designed even as the current version is being launched. Everything becomes obsolete and the only way to keep thriving is to accept that and adapt. We have to go with it.

And yet, we don't, do we? We are so reluctant to change that we're not willing to give up beliefs even when they're clearly painful, even when they're obviously getting in our own way. What gives? Are we, as a species, insane? I mean, it would explain a lot... But no. We're not crazy. We simply have some, what I call, 'core beliefs' that are getting in our way.

A core belief is a general, underlying belief that governs how we form and interact with smaller, more specific beliefs.

Core beliefs are to normal beliefs what your operating system is to the software you install on top of it.

Beliefs come in all shapes and sizes. Your belief about which coffee is best won't affect your life nearly as much as a belief of unworthiness will. The beliefs that affect us the most are the core beliefs we have about how the world works and how we fit into it. When these beliefs are outdated and obsolete, they will cause the most 'damage', because they affect us and can keep us stuck in smaller limiting beliefs. A limiting core belief can cause you to hang on to a smaller limiting belief, even when you become aware of that smaller belief and the fact that it clearly makes no sense.

In other words, if the core filter is for shoes, and the secondary filter is for blue shoes, getting rid of the secondary filter (blue) in order to look for jackets won't work. You're still only going to see shoes.

Case study: The world is full of douchebags

Meet Sue, a woman with a core belief of unworthiness.

At some point in her life, Sue decided that she's not good enough – this is her core belief. This core filter causes her to only see search results that match her vibration. For example, Sue exclusively meets men who treat her like crap. She takes full responsibility for their behaviour, seeing their actions towards her as proof of her unworthiness. After all, if she were somehow 'better', they'd be nicer to her, right?

So, Sue only has experiences with a rather small pool of men (only douchebags), and therefore any conclusion she comes to will be based on this limited data. After a couple of awful relationships and some even more awful dates, Sue decides that good-looking guys are not only douches (because

ALL men in her reality are douches), they're also liars. Every good-looking guy she's dated (she's dated three of them) has lied, so she concludes that this applies to ALL hotties. Now, she's not only settling for guys who treat her like crap, but also for unattractive (to her) guys that treat her like crap, in an attempt to at least not be lied to. Basically, she's doing her best to choose the lesser of the evils.

Now, let's say that Sue has begun to study Deliberate Receiving. *She figures out that she has the false belief that all hot men are liars and comes to a new conclusion: hot men don't have a monopoly on lying, and liars don't have a monopoly on hotness. In other words, there are men who lie who are not hot and there are men who are hot who don't lie. As she releases that secondary filter, hot men fill her dating pool again; she's no longer limited to just the unattractive guys. The only problem is that they're still all douchebags! This could, and often will, lead Sue to question her new decision, and revert back to dating unattractive men in an attempt to avoid the underlying, liar-generating belief.*

Of course, if Sue isn't doing this work deliberately, it's entirely possible that she'll never let that secondary belief go (never mind the deeper belief). If she doesn't acknowledge that she has a filter in place – that there are options available that she isn't currently seeing – then she'll only ever look at that pool of douchebags and come to conclusions based on what she sees. It would never occur to her that her observations might be wrong, that good-looking guys who aren't liars even exist. In this way, the core belief of unworthiness would be perpetuating the secondary belief of hot liars. Basically, you can only ever base your assumptions and decisions on what you see, on the evidence you have, unless you're willing to acknowledge that there's a lot more evidence than you're currently aware of;

evidence to support ANY perspective, in fact, and are willing to
go looking for it. You cannot see what you don't believe CAN
be there.

You can't become a match to a frequency
that you won't even acknowledge exists.

Limiting core beliefs can actually help in the formation of new
beliefs that do serve us, but only when seen through the lens of
a deeper, larger limiting belief. Sue's secondary belief did serve
her on some level – she filtered out the biggest liars. She chose
the lesser of two evils, in her view – between good-looking
guys who were douchebags and huge liars, and unattractive-
looking guys who were douchebags but not such huge liars. In
her mind, a douchey non-liar is better than a douchey liar, even
if he's not as good-looking.

Core beliefs can help form and keep us stuck in secondary
beliefs that make no sense, unless seen through the filter of the
core belief. In this way, larger beliefs set up a support structure
for smaller beliefs, creating a stable belief structure. The more
stable a belief structure, the harder it is to shift.

Before you go and get all depressed, let me point out two
things:

1. This same concept applies to positive beliefs and
   manifestations as well. A positive core belief will cause new
   positive beliefs to be formed, and will influence you to react
   in a better-feeling way to the manifestations that come
   into your reality, setting you up for a new, more positive
   Progression of a Manifestation. Positive core beliefs create
   the basis of a stable belief structure just as well as negative
   core beliefs. Remember it's a mechanical process. It doesn't
   care if you use it for 'good' or 'evil'.

2. Beliefs can be changed. Programs can be upgraded. Hard
    drives can be scrubbed clean.

How, exactly, do you go about doing that? Well, that's precisely
what we'll discuss in the next chapter.

Chapter 6

The Four Crappy Core Beliefs We All Share

Our beliefs, all of them, are nothing more than automated decisions, freeing us up from having to think about every detail of our lives, *all the time*. They are like software programs we've installed to help us function in this physical reality. Our limiting beliefs are simply outdated programs – software that once served us well, but no longer does. And just as software can be uninstalled and replaced, so can our beliefs. In this chapter we'll explore exactly how to do that, as well as which core beliefs (the granddaddies of all beliefs) can and probably are sabotaging our efforts to do so.

Changing limiting beliefs (or upgrading our programming) is a topic that's been, in my opinion, so overcomplicated that many people have given up altogether. I can't tell you how many times I've been asked to coach those who have read every book and tried every technique, only to be stuck still exactly where they don't want to be, feeling worse than ever. They've often come to the conclusion that this stuff just doesn't work or, even worse, it doesn't work for *them*, in particular. They'll ask, 'What am I doing wrong?' or heartbreakingly, 'What's wrong with me?' There's nothing wrong with them; they've simply gotten too caught up in the techniques rather than the process itself.

Now, don't get me wrong; there are a lot of different, amazing tools we can use to do inner work. I'm even sharing my favourite ones with you in this book. But in my experience, if you don't understand the basics of WHAT a technique is actually supposed to do and the underlying reason WHY it works, if you don't understand the process, you're pretty much just poking around in the dark… with a very small stick. Wearing noise-cancelling headphones. With your entire body wrapped in bubble wrap… and the target is moving. You're very, very likely to fail, is what I'm saying.

It's the difference between learning how to use a hammer and being taught how construction works, including which tools should be used for which job and why. Once you understand what really needs to happen, you can even jury-rig a solution, should you not have access to your tools in that moment. (You could use a knife instead of a screwdriver, for example.) If all you know is how to use a hammer, you're going to be up poop creek without a paddle when you're faced with a loose screw. If you try to use the hammer, you might conclude that the tool itself is useless (it's not, when used with nails), that you just don't know how to hammer (actually, even an expert hammerer would not be of any use in this moment), or that you're simply not meant to enjoy the grandeur of construction. So, while techniques, which are simply tools, are great, I'd rather teach you the underlying process.

So, here's the simple, elegant explanation of how to change a belief. Ready?

If all beliefs are simply decisions we made, conclusions we reached and opinions we have adopted as 'truth', it stands to reason that we could change any belief by simply making a new decision, coming to a new conclusion or forming a new opinion. And well, that's exactly how it works.

☕ Five Basic Steps to Changing Any ☕ Belief and Releasing Resistance

You can, in fact, change any belief by,

1. Recognizing that your current belief is based on an incomplete set of data.

2. Opening up your mind to the idea that more data, much of which will NOT support your *current* perspective, exists.

3. Deciding which perspective you'd like to adopt (or just how you want that perspective to feel).

4. Looking for the evidence to support that new, wanted perspective.

5. Gathering enough of that supporting data so that you can accept this new perspective as 'truth'.

This little five-step process, which you'll find repeated in Appendix III *(see page 246)* has the power to change your life. These five simple steps actually incorporate a huge shift in many of our society's core beliefs. They represent a fundamental change in perspective. But before we can break down and dissect our core beliefs, we have to recognize the prerequisite to deliberately receiving our reality, without which these five steps aren't even possible:

We must be *willing* to acknowledge that another perspective, a better-feeling perspective, exists, even if we're not yet able to see it.

Remember, you can't become a match to a frequency that you won't even acknowledge exists. You can't take conscious control of your hologram unless you're willing to acknowledge that control is possible. You can't fully master the game unless you're willing to admit that it is, in fact, a game.

Willingness is a concept that runs like a thread throughout this work. We have free will and so everything we do is a choice. Therefore, everything we do requires the willingness to do it, to face the outcome of what we're doing. As we pull back the curtain more and more on the mechanics of how reality actually works, as we dig into the process further and further – and especially as we begin to apply it to our physical lives – we are required at each step to provide willingness.

The Four Crappy Core Beliefs

Now, this might sound like a no-brainer. After all, if you weren't willing to change, why would you even be reading this book? Only, let's be honest. There are a lot of people (and this is true for all of us at some point in our lives) who dream of change, who want change, who even demand change, but who aren't actually *willing* to make a change. Wanting something and being actually willing to let it in are two different things. To bring it back into the realm of our Amazon analogy from Chapter 3 (*see page 39*), it's the difference between ordering something and actually taking delivery of it. If you refuse to accept the package, there's nothing Amazon can do.

But while willingness is a prerequisite to using any reality-shifting technique successfully, it is, by itself, not enough. We've actually adopted several core beliefs in our society that will block this process from working, which need to be addressed before we can become truly Deliberate Receivers.

Here are the four *crappy core beliefs* that tend to get in the way of us applying the Five Basic Steps to Changing Any Belief and Releasing Resistance:

Crappy Core Belief #1: There is only one truth

Much of our society runs on the premise that someone's got to be right, making everyone else wrong. There is only one truth and, when you find it, it's your responsibility to make sure everyone else finds it, too. In fact most conflicts, wars and disagreements are caused by people insisting that, first, their view is the single, correct one; and, second, that everyone else must now agree or be destroyed/banished/shamed into compliance.

Except, here's the thing; as I explained earlier, we're all sort of 'wrong' all the time. Every opinion is based on an incomplete amount of data. Every. Single. One. And that's OK. We are not meant to agree. This game is set up for diversity, not standardization and uniformity. Why do you think there's so much diversity in the world, anyway? Each of us has access to a (sometimes only slightly) different set of data. Each one of us can only see, experience and process so much. If we tried to take in every single detail that is possible to experience, we'd go bonkers. Have you ever tried to remember, let's say, 20 things on a shopping list, only to forget about half? Now consider what it would be like to keep track of an infinite amount of stuff. Does that sound even remotely fun to you? Our brains would shut down. We'd lose the ability to interact with each other or even to be consciously aware. We'd just be sitting there processing, seemingly comatose, and we still wouldn't even scratch the surface of perceiving what's possible. Our human-brain computers aren't designed for this purpose, in fact just the opposite.

We are perfectly designed to observe and experience one unique perspective at a time. We're not built to multitask, which isn't actually possible. We cannot fully focus on two things at once, but we can switch back and forth rapidly, sort of splitting our focus between the two, often half-assing each one, but never truly doing either one justice. We are focusing machines, able to immerse ourselves in any experience to the degree that it blocks out all other possibilities. In other words, even though our perspective is always, by design, limited, this limitation allows us to experience any set of narrowed-down data FULLY.

When we experience a perspective fully, to the exclusion of any other thoughts, when we engage in a full-sensory experience (meaning that we are completely aware of our senses), we enter into a state that's often referred to as being completely in the NOW. This is our natural state. This is when we are at the height of our focusing power. This is when we step outside of space and time (which is why time can speed up or slow down in this state). This is 'the zone'.

When we are purely in the NOW, we are observing and experiencing, and nothing else. We are not judging. We are not concluding or deciding. We are not processing. We are simply letting the experience be what it is. And because we're not offering any of those behaviours of resistance in this state, because we're completely in a state of allowing (letting it be what it is without judgement), we are, invariably, feeling good.

Deciding that there is only one truth is the complete antithesis to being in the NOW. It goes against the very fabric of how reality is constructed and what we're here for and how we are designed. When we're in the NOW, we are experiencing a set of narrowed-down data (narrowed down enough so that it leads to a singular experience), and this experience is meaningful. We resonate with it. It makes sense to us. We have clarity. We can feel its importance, its significance.

But then, we decide that this feeling must mean that THIS is the ONE truth, the one perspective that applies to all.

Only, it can't be. By our very design, we each have a different perspective. We each look at a different set of data. We each have a unique experience of that data. The real value lies in fully experiencing that data – all of it, something that no one can do alone. Collectively, however, we have a far better chance.

Think of it this way: You're in a group of ten people, and all of you want to know what every part of the world is like. You have two options:

1. You can each spend years and years travelling around the world, trying to get to know as many cultures as possible. But, even after a lifetime of travelling, you wouldn't have even come close to seeing the entire globe.

2. Or, you could each choose a section of the world to explore fully, and then get together and share your experiences via stories, pictures and videos.

Which option do you think would yield the most complete results? Which one would lead you to getting to know the most about the world's cultures? The second one, of course: ten people can accomplish far more than one person when they work as a team and share their experiences with each other.

Diversity exists because it has to – we are each designed to experience a section of reality and then grow by sharing the data we've observed and processed (experienced) with each other. Our different cultures, religions, backgrounds, geographical locations, genders, sexual preferences and belief systems are what make our unique perspectives possible. They are what shape many of the filters through which we each experience reality.

When we try to force someone to see things our way, we are ignoring this integral part of the game's design, which is why it never works. You can't force someone to see things your way, because it's impossible for them to do so. They can only ever see things their way. Now, you could come to the same conclusion based on different sets of data, and when that happens, it's very exciting (which is why we love it so much), but we can't manipulate each other into doing so. What's more, in our desperate quest for uniformity, we completely miss out on all the amazing data we can share with each other, and the expanded view of the Universe that comes with it.

The Five Basic Steps to Changing Any Belief and Releasing Resistance depend on the recognition that there is no one truth, but that we each have our own, and that we get to (and really have to) change that truth frequently. Your opinion is not THE truth; it is YOUR truth (for now…). Every single perspective is really just an opinion (or you can call it a theory or even hypothesis, if you like) based on incomplete data. As you gather more data, your opinion will (and should) change. This is how we grow and evolve. And, of course, if you're willing to acknowledge this for your own set of beliefs, then you have to do so for everyone else, as well.

Crappy Core Belief #2: We can't get what we want

The idea that sometimes, often – hell, more often than not – we can't get what we want, is a pervasive one. Many people operate on the premise that life is hard and full of disappointment (disappointment is the norm), but that if we're lucky or we work hard enough, we can get a glimpse of the good stuff every once in a while. Now, people will have a lot of secondary beliefs based on this one, which help to justify the core belief, such as 'I can't get what I want *because I don't deserve it*', or '*because I'm not worthy*', etc., but the core belief that builds that structure is the conclusion that we're playing an unwinnable game.

But why in the hell would we ever conclude something like that? I don't remember making that decision. Do you?

Keep in mind that not all of your beliefs (good or bad) stem from observations and decisions that you, personally, made. In fact, most of your beliefs (useful *and* outdated) were handed to you in a big old bundle of software when you were born and during the first seven years of your life. Your parents, your family, your culture, your society, even your geographical location all played a part in which programs you downloaded automatically. So, somewhere down the line, someone came to a conclusion about life based on incomplete data, and decided that this conclusion was 'true'. Coupled with the belief that there is only one 'truth', like-minded people banded together and began to convert others. Now, while you can't force someone to agree with you (you can only force them to act like it), you can begin to teach the new, impressionable generation that your limited, faulty conclusion is 'just the way it is'.

During our first six to seven years of life, we're like sponges. We just accept everything (or almost everything) as truth, as a given. We learn how the world works from our surroundings, mostly energetically (we just match the vibrations of those around us), but also through our observations. We soak up the beliefs of our elders. We're like wide-open funnels that all the beliefs in our family and culture just get dumped into. And since most people don't know that they can deliberately clean up their vibration before they pass it on to their kids, we pass on all the crappy beliefs right along with the useful ones. So, after a few generations, a belief can become completely indoctrinated into a society, even if the society that spawned it didn't unanimously agree.

At this point, many people want to get into a discussion about how limiting beliefs were spread, who did the indoctrinating (the church, the education system, or politicians, for example), and what their motives were. And while I'm not discounting the idea that there were (and are) some mean and horrible human beings running around, doing their best to spread limiting beliefs to the masses in order to make them more controllable or so they can feel more powerful or whatever, I'm not going to spend any time giving any energy to that perspective. To me, it's much more useful to acknowledge that all beliefs are:

- Simply observations.

- Changeable (each of us has the power to change our beliefs and therefore our reality).

The douchebags of the world can do what they want; I don't have to choose to bring any of that into my hologram. And neither do you.

At some point in our human history, someone observed that some people had more than others, and the concept of unfairness was born, simply because they couldn't figure out why that was. And from a place of powerlessness, a place of wanting something and not knowing how to get it, they concluded that most of the time, we're not going to get what we want.

Holding on to this perspective, however, is like saying that we can't drive cars now because we didn't know how they worked in the 1500s, or that we can't use computers because there was a time in our history when they didn't exist. Just because some dude a few thousand years ago couldn't figure out how the mechanism of reality works, doesn't mean we have to continue to operate from that perspective today. We have evolved. We know a lot more now than we knew then. We have access to a lot more data.

It's now easier than ever to get what you want. Get on your computer, order something off the Internet, type in your credit card number, sit back and wait for the goodies to show up at your house. You don't even have to get dressed.

Around the globe, 18-year-olds are launching billion-dollar companies. People are getting rich and happy doing things they love, travelling the world with their kids and living their dreams. We have more examples than ever that we can, indeed, get what we want. But we do have to be willing to believe it, or at least be open to the possibility.

What if you did, actually, get everything you've ever wanted? Most people won't even consider that thought, because it's too painful. They're convinced that this isn't even a possibility – they've accepted this as truth and have never given it a second thought. Think about that for a second; we collectively, en masse, simply accepted the idea that life is about survival, not thriving, that happiness is for the lucky few and that it's better not to pursue your dreams to avoid the inevitable disappointment. And very few of us ever raised our hands and questioned the basis of that belief. Sure, we railed against it, against the unfairness of it all, but what if the whole foundation of this belief is false? What if we can get what we want, but we haven't been doing so in large part because we decided that we couldn't? What if all those super-successful people who've been telling us to follow our passions and that any one of us could make it weren't just taunting the unfortunate many, but were telling the truth the whole damn time?

The Five Basic Steps to Changing Any Belief and Releasing Resistance depends on the recognition that getting what you want is, at least, a possibility. Ask yourself if you actually believe that it is possible for you, or someone like you, to get what you want, even if you have no idea how it will come about. Are you *willing* even to entertain the idea that maybe, just maybe, you can and even will get what you want? Will you make that new choice today and keep making it until it becomes an automated decision?

Crappy Core Belief #3: Beliefs are not a choice

Like Crappy Core Belief #2, the idea that beliefs are not a choice goes hand in hand with Crappy Core Belief #1 – that there's only one truth. You'll see this limitation show up in all walks of life, including religion and science.

The funny thing about this Crappy Core Belief is that even though it's widespread, we don't actually have to rattle that structure too hard to make it fall apart like a house of cards. You see the belief that what we believe is not a choice (accepting a point of view as absolute fact, one we MUST agree with) only works one way. That is to say, we apply it to ourselves, and apply the exact opposite to anyone who disagrees with us.

Someone who fervently believes that God will smite them if they watch reality TV, for example, or someone who's decided that all socialists or democrats are idiots, will argue that their belief is the *right* one, and this is just the way it is. Furthermore, they'll insist they have no choice but to believe as they do, since any other belief is wrong, or heresy, or blasphemy, or dangerous or just plain stupid. And yet, anyone who doesn't believe as they do should just change their minds and accept the one 'truth', in other words, *your* incorrect belief is a choice, yet *my* totally correct one isn't. It's really the height of arrogance.

People who embody this belief don't even consider that the other person's point of view represents a valid choice, one that they, themselves might not choose to adopt, but a valid choice nonetheless. They see their opponents as having deliberately and consciously decided not to adopt the truth, but instead do something they blatantly know to be wrong. As you can imagine, these types of people see the world very much in terms of right and wrong, black and white.

At its heart, this belief invalidates free will. Again, if we are to have true free will, then all choices must be equally valid and equally choosable. Deciding that some (or most) of the options we have access to are actually invalid, that we will be punished for choosing them, or that doing so will bring about the destruction of humanity, or the decline of society, etc., makes free will impossible. You cannot have free will and limit choices at the same time.

Think about this: anyone who's ever changed their minds about anything has to admit that, even though they thought they were totally right at some point, they were proven wrong by the very fact that they gathered more data and came to a new conclusion, which contradicted their old perspective. With this acknowledgement has to come the recognition that if they were wrong once, it stands to reason that they could be wrong again. About anything. And they'd have to concede that they *chose* to adopt a new belief when it made sense to do so. With that concession, Crappy Core Belief #3 falls apart.

But, if this belief is so nonsensical and falls apart so easily, why do so many people hold on to it with white-knuckled desperation? This is where it gets a little bit more complicated. You see this core belief is actually intertwined with Crappy Core Belief #1 – that there is only one truth. Because we intrinsically know that there really isn't only one truth while trying to hold on to the idea that there is, we are always going to be at least a little bit insecure in our views. We can counteract this insecurity, and therefore stabilize the structure of Crappy Core Belief #1, by buying into the idea that we don't really have a choice in the matter and then blaming the whole debacle on God or logic or morality or [*insert whatever other reason you want to (mis-)use for this purpose here*].

You see, when you believe that there is only one right answer and having the wrong answer is a bad, bad thing (you're going to burn in hell, get ostracized by the community, die alone out on the tundra), your safety and security and possibly even survival lie in being right. No matter what. But, if you're not totally sure if *your* belief is actually the one, correct one, you're going to need either to concede that there is no one right belief, or you'll have to simply bully all those who disagree with you into submission. If no one is contradicting you, it proves that you're right. Right? You're much more likely to follow the second method (bullying) than the first, not because it's your nature to do so, but because you were taught that this is the way we've always done it. So, you find others that agree with you and you fight against anyone who so much as questions whatever conclusion you're defending. The more afraid you are of being wrong, the more vigorously you'll fight. You might even try to pass laws that forbid any point of view other than your own. In severe cases, you'll kill those who won't openly support your *rightness*.

This belief, fragile as it is, actually stabilizes a whole host of other limiting beliefs. It's what makes it possible for us to hang on to all kinds of illogical conclusions that haven't served us since the Stone Age. If only one belief can be right (meaning it's not really a choice) and you HAVE TO BE RIGHT in order to survive, then you'll spend all your time defending your beliefs rather than exploring them in order to figure out if they are, indeed, the beliefs you want to keep holding on to.

The Five Basic Steps to Changing Any Belief and Releasing Resistance depend on recognizing that you *can* choose what to believe and that you *can* change your perspective at will. You can't decide which perspective to adopt, if you don't consider any other perspectives as valid. You can't change your beliefs, as long as you're afraid that doing so will damn you or kill you or ruin your life. Luckily, if you're willing to apply even a teensy bit of logical thinking to this belief, it will fall apart like wet toilet paper.

All perspectives are valid and meant to be shared and discussed, not debated. Our ability to choose our perspectives (free will) is one of our greatest gifts, and one of the main building blocks of the mechanism of the reality game.

Crappy Core Belief #4: I'll believe it when I see it

We live in an evidence-based, or 'show me', world. 'Let me see it and then I'll believe it,' we say. And many, especially the intelligent among us, would argue this is a good system. After all, we don't want to believe just any old thing, right? We don't want to be stupid and believe that unicorns and dragons roam the uncharted hills of England. Or do we?

Stay with me here, I promise not to go off the deep end to try and convince you that Big Foot is real. What I am advocating is that we never rule any possibility out. After all, you can't prove a negative (you cannot prove, beyond a shadow of a doubt, that Big Foot is NOT real…).

Let's do a little review of how we create our holographic reality.

We focus on something and begin to vibrate at the frequency that this thing represents to us. As we focus on it more, the Law of Attraction causes more energy of that same frequency to join in (it grows) and more and more evidence of that frequency shows up. As we experience this evidence, a desire for something even better is born. We can realize this desire or not.

This desire will, in that moment, not have a physical representation in our reality. It will merely be an idea, a concept. It's real in the non-physical, but we have to attune ourselves to its representational frequency in order to experience it. In other words, we have to be willing to focus on something for which we currently have no evidence. We have to be willing to believe it before we can 'see' it. If we don't, we're not realizing our desire, and will continue to have the same experience over and over again. We *receive* the same reality over and over again. We're stuck in the pit, running relentlessly back and forth.

This isn't as out there as it sounds. True scientists are dreamers. They have to be. A scientist looking for a breakthrough has to believe that a solution exists, even if they currently don't know what it is – even if *no other human in the history of the world* has ever found that solution.

In fact, this is why we have the tools of 'imagination' and 'faith' in our reality-manifesting tool belt. 'What's that?' I hear you ask. You didn't realize that imagination and faith were tools? Well, they are. You see, *nothing is wasted*. Nothing in your reality is there by chance, by mistake or by coincidence. This applies to the kid kicking the back of your seat on the plane, as well as your characteristics and abilities. Everything and I mean *EVERYTHING* has its purpose.

If we consider that this is NOT an unwinnable game, that this game is, in fact, very, very winnable, then doesn't it make sense that we would have all the tools we need in order to be successful? Well, it turns out that we do. Two of those tools are imagination and faith.

We often treat imagination as a childhood luxury that has no place in the serious adult world, but it's actually the mechanism by which we are able to attune ourselves to frequencies that have no representation in our perceivable reality. In fact, this is the way in which we create a new reality, one that's different from what we can currently see. When we reach for a solution that doesn't yet exist, we use imagination to line up with it. At first, we might only imagine a very rough solution, a generally positive outcome (or just the idea that a solution exists), but as we continue to focus and let the Law of Attraction do its thing, we will be able to imagine the outcome we want in greater and greater detail. Without the tool of imagination, we couldn't ever create anything other than what's already in our reality. We truly do imagine our world into being.

Faith is the tool that allows us to believe that this solution, which we currently have no evidence to support, can and will actually come about. Without faith, we wouldn't be able to fully attune ourselves to the frequency of what we've imagined. Imagination without faith is fantasy. If you actually want to experience something in your physical reality, you'll have to have both.

Unfortunately, faith has come to mean something else entirely in our society. When we talk about faith, we usually mean 'blind faith', meaning that we should believe in something that we *totally* don't currently believe, without *any supporting evidence whatsoever*. But faith doesn't work that way. Remember that no one can convince you of anything; you have to choose to be convinced. Let's look at the ultimate example of faith – a belief in God. People that truly believe in God do not do so simply because someone told them to. Those who were simply told to have faith might try to believe in God and even defend that belief to the death to avoid facing the idea that they're really not sure if God exists, but if their own personal criteria for adopting that belief haven't been met, they won't.

Someone who *truly* believes in God and has no need to defend that belief (their belief is not shaken by someone who doesn't share it) has invariably had some kind of experience that 'proved' it to them. They've been presented with enough evidence to allow themselves to fully choose this belief.

Now, I know what you're thinking. Didn't I just contradict myself? Didn't I just say that you have to believe it to see it, and then give you an example of how seeing it can cause you to believe it? Nope. Allow me to clarify.

Beliefs, especially core beliefs that affect how you see the world and your place in it, aren't formed (or changed) in an instant. While some smaller beliefs may have resulted from a snap decision, most of them will have been adopted *incrementally*. The process of forming beliefs is, once again, a progressive one. I hope that you're beginning to see a pattern here. Nothing in our reality happens instantaneously or in isolation. Nothing just appears or disappears. There's always, *ALWAYS*, a Progression. Reality grows into being, and manifestations wax and wane. They gravitate in and out of our reality. You're never going to have a negative manifestation that wasn't preceded by negative emotions and loads of negative synchronicities. You're never going to be able to push something out of your reality, but as you focus on something else, you'll be able to grow that new thing and watch the old, unwanted thing wither.

Beliefs are the same way. When you imagine a new solution into being, you do so incrementally. When you're focused on a problem and you switch to a solution, you'll be switching from one Progression of a Manifestation (*see page 48*), which may be well under way, to a new one. In other words, you'll be starting off at stage 1 of the new Progression. At first, you'll only be able to imagine the solution in its most general form – an outline of what you want. Basically, you'll begin by imagining that a solution has been found. You won't be able to see exactly how that solution will look, what it will entail, or how it will come about. You'll simply begin by seeing the problem fixed, which will feel good (your feedback that you're on the right track). If you try to see a more specific solution, you'll be trying to jump ahead in the Progression (to stage 3 and beyond), and you'll lose your alignment – it won't feel good.

Think of it this way: let's say that you're looking through a telescope in order to spy on someone across the city. You're currently watching the screen of your target's computer, having zoomed in so narrowly that you can even see what he's writing. Now, let's say that you need to find a new target, in a completely different building. If you try simply to swivel that telescope around a bit in order to find your new target, while continuing to zoom in that narrowly, you'll see nothing but a blur. Finding that new target will be like trying to find a straw-coloured needle in a haystack. If, however, you take your eye off the viewfinder and just look at the city's skyline (a broader, more general view), you can find the building where your new target works and point your telescope at that. Now, you can use the telescope on a less specific setting, to find the right row of windows, and then narrow your focus to the correct window, the desk and finally the computer screen.

In other words, if you want to change targets (shift from the problem to the solution), you'll have to back off, take a broader view to reorient yourself, and then focus in on that new target gradually. If you try to focus too narrowly too soon, you'll lose your place and things will get blurry and frustrating.

Thanks to the Law of Attraction, this narrowing of the focus happens automatically. As you activate a specific frequency, the LOA will bring you ever more specific manifestations that match it. But you have to allow that process to unfold instead of trying to jump ahead in the Progression. You can't find the specific window if you haven't taken the time to find the right building first. You can't find the right desk if you haven't taken the time to find the correct window, and so on. Each step leads to the next.

Now, let's get back to how the tool of faith fits into all of this. As you keep imagining the idea of the solution and how it will feel, more and more details will manifest and the picture will become more and more vivid. You only need to have enough faith to believe in whatever it is your imagination currently has access to. You don't need to have 'blind' faith in a solution that you can't yet imagine, and your imagination will only ever be able to access easily the next stage in the Progression of a Manifestation, but not much beyond that. To put it another way, you only need to have faith that you can find that other building, not that you can find that new target's computer screen. After that, you only need to have faith that you can find the window, and so on.

Let's say that you feel unworthy and you'd like to change that belief. Blind faith would require you to reach for the exact opposite: that you are worthy, and do your best to believe it. So, you chant affirmations of total worthiness. And... nothing happens. In fact, you may even start to feel worse. The problem is that you're reaching too far; you're not respecting the Progression of a Manifestation. If, however, you begin to change your belief incrementally, you use your imagination to find a solution that feels good, no matter how general, and you have faith in the fact that this solution could come about (perhaps 'I believe that I will, eventually, feel better'), you'll make a lot more headway. We'll be spending a lot more time on the process of exactly how to shift a belief incrementally in Chapters 10 and 11, but for now, remember that it's an incremental process, that everything is a Progression, and that you only have to apply imagination and faith to the next step in that Progression.

Once you truly understand the progressive nature of reality, it will become easier to adopt the perspective that you have to believe it to see it. After all, the physical evidence can't manifest until you match the frequency that will allow you to perceive it, but if you understand how to attune yourself to that frequency bit by bit, allowing each piece of evidence to fuel the creation and reception of the next one, you'll have all the knowledge you need to shape your reality into anything you want.

The Five Basic Steps to Changing Any Belief and Releasing Resistance depend on the recognition that there is more to your reality than you can currently, physically perceive, and that you can manifest this 'more' by incrementally building your faith in its *physical* existence. You cannot look for the evidence needed to allow you to adopt fully a new belief, if you're not willing to believe in at least the existence of that evidence.

Let's recap...

We've now explored:

- What vibration is.

- What we really mean when we talk about matching the frequency of something (representational frequency).

- How your desires are born.

- That your emotions are a feedback system, which helps you to attune yourself to what you want.

- The mechanics of the Law of Attraction.

- How you choose what you want to manifest in your reality.

- How manifestations actually become physical.

- How you automatically set up your next manifestation through your reaction to the current one.

- What resistance is and the basic requirements for shifting it.

Are you ready to run out in the 'real world' and start applying this knowledge? Not just yet.

You see, even though I've just dissected four of the biggest core beliefs that our society holds and which you were most certainly programmed with to some degree, you're not exactly going to be limiting-belief-free now. In fact, out of the millions or possibly billions of beliefs you hold, a small but significant percentage will always be obsolete and need to be replaced. I've shown you the basic process of how to shift a limiting belief (see page 77), but what I haven't yet done is teach you how to actually find those beliefs.

You could, of course, just read a ton of books, exposing yourself to loads of different perspectives and evidence that supports them, in the hope that you will recognize some of your own limiting beliefs in someone else's story. This is a valid technique, just a really, really slow one. You have to read a lot of books, and there's never any guarantee that what you're reading will actually contain something useful to you. It's a bit like trying to find a defective needle in a stack of needles.

But, if you understand how reality actually works, and you now do, you can use that knowledge to get those pesky limiting beliefs to yell, 'Yoooohoooo! Here we are!' In other words, instead of hunting through all your beliefs in an attempt to find the limiting ones, you can make them come to you. We'll discuss how to do that in Chapter 9, but before we can do that, we'll have to delve deeper. Way, WAY deeper.

Part II

THE NITTY-GRITTY

Chapter 7

Introducing the Spectrum of Empowerment

Now that we've explored the basic mechanics of how reality works and how you, the powerful creator in charge of your reality, can control it, it's time to delve into the nitty-gritty of the machine. So far, you've gained enough understanding to begin to make some changes to your world. You know the basic rules of the game, and have an inventory of most of the tools that are at your disposal. You know to focus on something positive, to pay attention to your feelings and to do your best to feel good. Best of all, you know exactly why those things are important. Now it's time to give you the advanced manual, the understanding that will allow you to find any resistance and release it with surgical precision, as well as fine-tune your focus on what you want so that it will manifest in your reality effortlessly and easily.

It's time to delve into the heart of Deliberate Receiving, explore our emotions and what they really mean, and learn how to shift from a worse-feeling emotion to a better-feeling one.

As I mentioned in Chapter 2, humanity is in the process of crossing the threshold from the Old World, which is about pain minimization, into the New World, which is about pleasure maximization. This shift and the corresponding points of focus (pleasure vs. pain) can be mapped out on a spectrum, which I call the 'Spectrum of Empowerment'.

Imagine a basic number line: a horizontal line with numbers where zero marks the spot in the middle, with positive numbers (1, 2, 3, etc.) ascending to the right, and negative numbers (−1, −2, −3, etc.) descending to the left. Don't worry, this is about as math-*y* as we're going to get. I've even made you a diagram to make it easier; see Fig. 1 below.

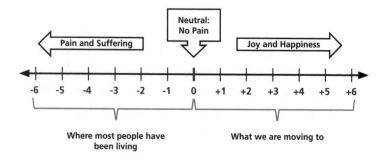

Fig 1: The Spectrum of Empowerment

On this number line, zero represents neutral – the point at which there is no pain, but also no pleasure. The negative end of the Spectrum represents the Old World, where we are more concerned about what is wrong with the world, and decisions are made based on what's less painful. The lower the number (−10 is lower than −5), or the further to the left you go down the Spectrum, the worse you feel.

The positive end of the Spectrum represents the New World, where we're focused on what's right with the world and how to make it even better, and decisions are made based on what feels best. The higher the number, or the further to the right you go up the Spectrum, the better you feel.

Living on the Spectrum

Throughout human history, we've tended towards operating in the negative side of the Spectrum. We, as a society, have been (and still are) generally focused on the problem (what's wrong?) instead of the solution (how we want it to look instead). We've been assuming that pain is a necessary part of life, even taking pride in our ability to put up with a crap load of it ('My pain threshold is SOOOOOO high, I can work 80-hour weeks! While having the flu! And taking care of five kids! Who also have the flu! No amount of suffering can stop me!'). And, for the most part, our goal has been to get to zero – what many people thought and still think, is the highest possible goal. In other words, we've been doing our best just to reduce and, dare we even hope, to eliminate the pain.

Most of our institutions are still set up this way. Our medical and psychological systems are both designed to take us from non-functioning to functioning, from ill to not-so ill, from in pain to not in pain. But a lack of pain is not the same as a presence of pleasure. Just because you don't feel bad, doesn't mean you feel good. To put it more bluntly, deciding not to eat Jalapeño peppers in order to avoid flames shooting out of your mouth (and later an opening that's far, far worse), is not the same as eating chocolate. Not even close.

Neutral is just the middle of the Spectrum. There's a whole other side, a whole other world to be explored. This is the side of the Spectrum that more and more people are waking up to.

But you don't have to wait for them to wake up in order to make that shift. You see, the Spectrum works on a macro as well as a micro level. It can be applied to society, a group of people, a culture, a family, one person, and even a single moment in that person's life. As a society, we may be operating on the negative side of the Spectrum. Our news outlets are almost exclusively interested in bad news. Our politicians are much more interested in war than peace. People, in general, spend a lot more time bitching and complaining than praising and appreciating. But you, as an individual, are not required in any way to buy into that. You can choose to be at any point on the Spectrum, no matter where your neighbours or colleagues or family are. Society could be miserable, while you're a Happy Shiny Puppy. Notice that you don't have to be happy *because of* their misery; you simply do not need to share in it.

What's more, you could be on one side of the Spectrum one day, and on the other side the next day. You could be at a −3 on one issue, and a +2 on another issue. As I said, it applies on a macro (grand, societal) scale, and a micro (teensy-weensy, individual, even moment-to-moment) scale.

There is no good place or bad place to be on the Spectrum. This is why I'm using a mathematical number line to represent this concept. Maths, bless its little heart, knows no judgement. One number is no 'better' or 'worse' than another. They're all just numbers. A 'negative' number is not bad or detrimental. In this context, the word 'negative' doesn't mean unwanted. It's just a way to signify which side of the Spectrum you're on. It's a way to pinpoint your vibrational location, if you will.

At this point, I want to make something very, very clear: whenever we speak about vibration, we always have to remember that it's completely *relative*. Remember from Chapter 4 (*see page 45*) how a 'higher' vibration simply meant a more aligned one: meaning, one that felt better *to you*? The same concept applies here. In fact, it's *exactly* the same concept. When you focus on something that makes you feel better, you move up (or to the right on) the Spectrum. Your vibration therefore becomes 'higher' (but not necessarily higher than someone else's, just higher than it was before – for *you*). When you focus on something that makes you feel worse, you move down (or to the left on) the

Spectrum. Your vibration becomes 'lower' than it was before. So, when you hear teachers, including me, talking about 'raising your vibration', we're talking about moving up the Spectrum.

But why is this important? Why am I telling you about this Spectrum? For two reasons:

1. The Spectrum of Empowerment is actually the main framework of *Deliberate Receiving*. While I've introduced you to the very basic number line, I'm going to be filling in that framework with a lot more information before you reach the end of this book.

2. Where you are on the Spectrum not only determines how you feel, but which techniques you need to apply in order to feel better. This is why some people are best off just taking a nap to feel better, while others will get results by focusing on cleaning up some negative thoughts. This is why there seem to be so many contradictions in the advice given by different teachers. If you assume that all advice applies to everyone at any time, of course it's going to seem contradictory. And if you then apply a technique that isn't right for you in that moment, thinking it should work for you because it worked for someone else, and it doesn't help, you might easily think there's something wrong with you or the technique. When actually, all that's happened is that you didn't respect where you are in the Spectrum and choose your 'treatment' accordingly.

It's a bit like training for a marathon. If you've never run in your life and want to run a marathon, you don't start off by tackling 26 miles on your first day. You respect your current level of fitness and train accordingly. Now, of course, you could throw yourself on the ground and wail about how you wished you were in better shape, but that wouldn't help at all, would it? If you want to actually run that marathon, you have to figure out your current level of fitness, and then use the right type of training to take you from where you currently are to where you want to go. Trying to use the training regimen of someone in far better shape than you would actually be counterproductive. You'd probably get hurt and lose a lot of time to recovery (recovery consisting of sitting on the couch, insisting that you never wanted to run that marathon anyway, while cry-eating a tub of Ben and Jerry's). If you try to use a technique that's designed for a different part of the Spectrum than the one you're on, you're not only going to fail, it may actually make you feel worse (because now you feel like a failure on top of everything else).

This is why being aware of the Spectrum, and where you currently reside on it, is so important. But how can you tell where you are? Well, as it turns out, you can tell by the way you feel. Your emotions, that glorious feedback system, are tied directly to this Spectrum. Isn't that convenient? Each section of the Spectrum is associated with specific emotions. In order to determine where you are on the Spectrum, and therefore how to move on up that scale, you first have to identify and acknowledge how you currently feel.

Again, this may sound like kind of a 'duh!' point, but it's actually another one of those huge stumbling blocks that just about everybody trips over. Particularly those of us who tend to overthink stuff and are way too intellectual for our own good: we have the biggest tendency to fall on our faces when it comes to registering how we really feel. Splat! A little bit of knowledge can be a dangerous thing. A lot of knowledge without true understanding can be a debilitating thing. This is why I frequently work with those who have read every book, studied all the courses and know all the lingo by heart, but can't seem to actually apply that knowledge to the areas of their lives that are most important to them. In almost every one of those cases, at least part of the problem (usually the biggest part) stems from a failure to acknowledge where they truly are on the Spectrum.

Again, this is why I'm choosing a kind mathematical scale to represent this Progression. Maths doesn't judge and neither should you (geekiest bumper sticker ever…).

No emotion is 'bad'. They are all helpful messengers that are trying to help you get where you want to go.

The Spectrum of Empowerment and your emotions

In order to utilize the messages that our emotions are trying to give us, we have to understand what each of them means and where they lie on the Spectrum.

Before we map that out, however, let's just clarify one thing: just like your vibration and frequency and your opinion and perspective, this is all deeply personal and individual work. Even though I can give you a basic outline of what the emotions mean and where they fall on the Spectrum, in the end, how you might label where you are on the number line really comes down to your own definitions. For example, what some people call anger, others call rage. What some people call frustration, others call annoyance. *Tomayto, tomahto.*

I've addressed this issue by first giving you a definition of each emotion and then grouping similar emotions together on the Spectrum under a generic heading, instead of trying to map each one individually. For example, rage, hatred and jealousy are all in the same group, which I've called 'ANGER'. For some people, jealousy will feel less volatile than rage while, for others, hatred is more intense. But they're all in the same vicinity, and as far as pinpointing your location on the Spectrum, it's close enough. What's most important is that you don't blindly follow some graph, but rather, feel your way through this, being as aware of your emotions at every stage possible. You cannot *think* your way through this, no matter how hard you try. I know that seems a little bit paradoxical, since I'm the queen of explaining stuff (I mean, I *literally* wrote the book on it…). And while it's obviously really helpful to understand the mechanics of it all, when it comes to actually applying this understanding, you have to be willing to get your hands dirty (emotionally).

Let's begin by looking at the definition of emotions. Keep in mind that these are my definitions. If you don't agree with any of them, that's OK. Remember that, at its core, this is all about feeling better. If linking a definition to a different term helps you to do that, then go for it. These definitions will, however, help me explain the process of releasing even the most stubborn of limiting beliefs.

Definition of emotions

Boredom: The feeling of being idle, of not letting yourself move forwards. This feeling can actually occur at any point in the Spectrum.

Deep depression: A feeling of numbness caused by severely suppressed anger; of being disconnected from the self and the world. Nothing matters.

Total powerlessness: Like lying down and letting yourself get beaten, without having the strength or motivation to do anything about it.

Total despair: A feeling of deep, overpowering sadness; one step up from depression. Feeling trapped, having given up on the idea that anything can be done about it.

Shame: A feeling that you are wrong (as opposed to having done something wrong). You are bad in some way. Not good enough.

Guilt: A feeling that you have done something wrong. This is often coupled with shame ('I have done something wrong because there's something wrong with me'), but doesn't necessarily have to be.

Severe insecurity: The world is a hostile place and you are not safe. This emotion spans both depression and shame, depending on the severity of the insecurity (can you make yourself a little bit safe by appeasing others, or not at all?).

Fear: See *severe insecurity* (above) because they're the same thing.

Unworthiness: The feeling of not being good enough.

Self-blame: The feeling that everything is your fault, especially when others feel bad for any reason.

Fake gratitude: The feeling you get when you're trying to be grateful to some hostile power outside of yourself, either to appease them or because you've been told you should be. It's fake because being grateful out of obligation or in order to get something (even safety) is not gratitude. It's powerlessness and often a form of manipulation.

Resentment: The feeling you get when you are giving more than you actually want to give, doing things not because you want to, but out of obligation.

Blame (*blaming others*)**:** The feeling you get when you naturally turn your self-blame outwards, allowing the energy to flow out, rather than inwards (self-blame). Healthy when practised deliberately, constructively and *temporarily*.

Hatred (*intensified **blame***)**:** This happens when you've suppressed the anger and urge to ***blame*** for too long.

Revenge (*severely intensified **blame**, usually even more intense than **hatred***): This happens when you've suppressed the anger and urge to blame and hatred for too long.

Anger: The feeling you get when you're finally sick of the world beating you up, and you're ready to stand up and fight back. This emotion takes you out of powerlessness.

Rage (*intensified **anger***): Happens when you've suppressed anger for too long.

Jealousy: The feeling you get when you want something that someone else has, and believe that because they have it, you can't. Belief based on scarcity (there's only so much to go round).

Envy (*a lighter form of **jealousy***): Pure envy is simply wanting something that someone else has; it is jealousy without the component of scarcity.

Pessimism/negative expectation: A negative perspective, more trust in the fact that things will not work out rather than that they will.

Frustration: The feeling that you can and should receive what you want, but that it's just out of reach. A feeling of 'Why is this not working?!' Also a sign that you are trying to take action too soon and make something happen.

Discouragement (*a lighter form of **pessimism***): You still trust the negative more than the positive, but you're not really sure of it.

Contentment: Neutral, with a slightly positive focus. You are no longer feeling pain, but there's not yet much pleasure. Some people also use the word contentment to describe the state of appreciation, but for the sake of clarity, I'm going to be sticking with the 'neutral' definition.

Hope (*a 'lesser' form of **optimism***)**:** You are willing to trust the positive more than the negative, but aren't quite sure of it.

Optimism: You are willing to trust the positive more than the negative.

Gratitude (*a 'lesser' form of **appreciation***)**:** Appreciating what you have, but still being beholden to some outside power to some degree (i.e. 'I'm grateful that I received this from…') This is not to be confused with fake gratitude or appreciation, although many people use them interchangeably.

Positive expectation: The feeling of trusting that good things will happen. Can be dampened if the expectation is too specific.

Enthusiasm (*usually less controlling than **positive expectation***)**:** The feeling of trusting that good things will happen and looking forward to them.

Appreciation: Simply seeing the good in what is in your reality right now.

Celebration (**appreciation** *on steroids*)**:** Unconditional appreciation.

Love: The feeling of focusing on something with only appreciation.

Unconditional love: Focus on something with only appreciation, and without any need for the object of our focus to give anything back.

Joy: The feeling of being totally in the NOW.

Passion: The feeling of being totally in the NOW, engaged in inspired action.

Full empowerment: The knowledge that not only is everything always working out *for* you, but that everything happens in response to your vibration.

You may notice as I introduce you to the emotional groups that some of these emotions can actually fall into more than one group, depending on how the label (the word) is used. Once you understand the belief systems that underlie each emotional group (which we'll explore in Chapter 8), it will be easy for you to figure out exactly where you are on the Spectrum by how you feel, regardless of what label you give it.

The seven emotional groups in the Spectrum of Empowerment

Now, using Fig. 2 (*see opposite*), let's look at each of the emotional groups in turn. At the very 'bottom', you have emotional group 1, DEPRESSION (utter despair, deep depression and a feeling of total powerlessness). At the very 'top', you'll find emotional group 7, JOY (love, passion, joy, full empowerment and celebration).

So, the Spectrum takes us from 'total powerlessness' – a sense that random bad stuff just happens to us while there's nothing we can do about it – to 'full empowerment' – a sense of complete control over our reality, and a knowing that we can not only choose to experience whatever we want, but that we have the skill actually to do so. This is why it's called the Spectrum of *Empowerment*. Every emotional state in between these two extremes represents a different degree of empowerment.

When we shift from one emotion to another, we either become *more* empowered (which feels better), or *less* empowered (which feels worse).

Looking at Fig. 2, you may notice that the HOPE group is placed just to the right of the 'neutral point' (Zero Point). This is no mistake. Remember that the Zero Point is neutral (not bad, not good) and represents the dividing line between being problem-oriented and solution-oriented. These emotions of hope signify that you've crossed the threshold – you've raised your vibration

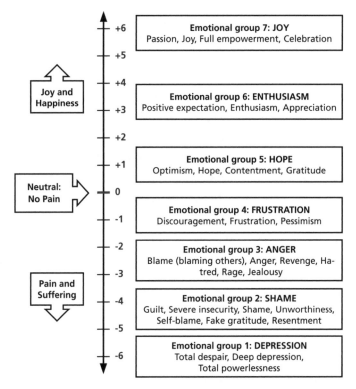

Fig. 2: Emotional groups in the Spectrum of Empowerment

to the point where you now have access to solution-oriented thoughts. But why wouldn't we have access to these types of thoughts throughout the whole Spectrum? Isn't that a design flaw? Wouldn't it be easier if we could access solutions from anywhere in the Spectrum? Well, actually you do, sort of. You see it's not that someone is keeping you from accessing those types of thoughts in the higher part of the Spectrum. They're always there for you to access. It's just that when you're vibrating at lower frequencies, you can't receive or experience those thoughts. You can't manifest them. Someone could be literally smacking you in the face with the solution you're looking for and you wouldn't recognize it as such.

If you've ever tried to give someone a solution to their problem, one that was glaringly obvious to you, and they just wouldn't hear of it, much to your frustration, you've experienced this phenomenon. They could not recognize the solution for what it was. It didn't make sense to them; it didn't resonate. Even if it was clear as day to you, they weren't hearing it the same way as you were. They didn't have your perspective. And that's what this is all about – perspective. If you're climbing a mountain, your view or perspective is going to change. The higher you go, the broader your view. Things that were totally invisible to you in the valley (lower vibration, limited view) become really clear and obvious when you're higher up (higher vibration, broader view). You have access to information, data and solutions that you simply couldn't observe in the valley. There's nothing wrong with being in the valley, but you can't expect to have the same view as you would on the mountaintop. If you want that view, you're going to have to go higher.

Again, let me reiterate my point about not judging (ah, judgement – that sneaky bastard will creep up on you). You are not being *rewarded* with more information for moving to the positive side of the Spectrum, just as you aren't being *punished* with lack of information for being on the lower side of the Spectrum. This would be like saying that you are being rewarded with running water for going into the bathroom and punished with lack of running water for going into the living room. If you know how to move from one side of the Spectrum to the other, and you know that it's not hard to get the broader view (clarity, solutions) you want, then you'll stop thinking in terms of negative Spectrum equals bad, and positive Spectrum equals good. You'll simply go where you need to go on the Spectrum in order to get the information or experience you want. The key is to stop throwing a tantrum because you're in the living room instead of the bathroom, or because you're currently angry instead of swimming in joy. Both serve their purpose. Just recognize where you are and plot a course to where you want to be.

In the next chapter, we'll take a look at each group of emotions and how they fit into the Spectrum in terms of empowerment, starting with the most painful emotions and working our way up (got to end on a high note…). I'll also be mapping out which belief system corresponds with each emotional group. Later, in Chapter 11, I'll show you how to move from one emotion to another and how to use this knowledge to attune yourself to the frequency of your choice.

Keep in mind that the Spectrum is fluid. No one permanently hangs out in any one spot. And while you'll usually occupy a certain range on the Spectrum (it's unlikely that you'll feel total passion in one moment and total depression the next), you can move about quite a bit within that range. So, while you may feel enthusiasm most of the time, you may feel anger on a certain issue. The key is not to demonize any one emotional group, but to recognize that all have value.

Why we're afraid of our negative emotions

In Chapter 4 we discussed how your feelings are the key to manifesting what you want, as opposed to manifesting what you don't want. The better you feel, the more aligned you are with the frequency of what you want. So, really, if you think about it, the secret to a happy life is simply to feel good. End of book. What's that you say? That's not enough? You've tried to feel better but couldn't? You'd feel better *if you just knew how*? You're getting annoyed at the fact that I'm putting everything in the form of a question? Fair enough.

While feeling better should really be a no-brainer, it clearly isn't. In Chapter 5 I explained that no one ever actually wants to be in pain. It may seem otherwise at times, because we insist on holding on to ideas that are painful, but it's only ever because we're avoiding something that we think will hurt even more. The only reason that we ever hold on to an idea that's painful is because we have a belief that causes us to think that this idea represents the best-feeling option we currently have access to. Our limiting beliefs cause us to stay in a painful state. So, it stands to reason that if we find out what these beliefs are and shift our perspective, we'll feel better.

But how are we supposed to figure out what our limiting beliefs are? Well, it turns out that our belief systems can be mapped to the Spectrum. When we're feeling an emotional response to something we're focusing on, that emotion doesn't just let us know if what we're focusing on is wanted (positive emotion) or unwanted (negative emotion), it also gives us clues as to what kind of belief system we're currently holding on to. Our emotions are pretty bad-ass in that way.

At this point, you may be tempted to think, 'Ah, so negative emotions are caused by limiting beliefs', but that's not entirely correct. You see, even if you had no limiting beliefs whatsoever, which isn't possible since all beliefs become, by design, limiting at some point (they become obsolete), you'd still have *some* negative emotion. Negative emotion is simply a feedback mechanism that lets you know that you're focusing on something unwanted, giving you the opportunity to notice that icky feeling and immediately shift your focus to something else. Your limiting beliefs are what cause you to keep on focusing in a way that triggers more and more negative emotion, as well as to ignore that feedback, no matter how uncomfortable it may get. So, technically speaking, while limiting beliefs don't cause negative emotion, they do greatly increase the amount of negative emotion that we feel. This may seem like a tiny distinction, but it's actually a pretty important one. As long as you think of negative emotion as a kind of punishment for having limiting beliefs, and as limiting beliefs as something you're doing 'wrong', you won't be able to receive the helpful messages your feelings have for you.

As I said, even if we had no limiting beliefs, we'd still have negative emotion. It would just be much, much milder and much shorter-lived than it currently is. Consider this: nature on our planet is one wise system. Fruits and vegetables, for example, taste best when they are the most nutritious. A banana doesn't fully develop its sweetness until it's completely ripe, at which stage it also has the most benefit for us, nutritionally. So, early man and woman didn't have to have degrees in nutrition in order to know which foods to eat in nature, they just had to follow their taste buds (this mechanism is still in place today, although the introduction of artificial foods has thrown that communication out of whack to a large degree. You can recover it, though, if you're willing to go back to natural foods). The foods that were bad for humans also smelt and tasted bad to us (rotten food, for example). So, the feedback mechanism of taste is a pretty handy one. If you try some new kind of food and don't like it, do you curse your taste buds, wishing your sense of taste would go away? Do you blame yourself for being some kind of failure for not liking this food? Or do you accept that your sense of taste has given you valuable information about this food and simply choose to eat something that tastes better?

Our emotions, all of them, are exactly like this. When you feel a negative emotion, it simply means that you're currently focusing on something you don't like. The idea is to stop doing that and focus on something else, instead of demonizing the emotion itself.

But, alas, demonize them we do (cue ominous music). In fact, we've been taught not only to keep our displays of emotions to a minimum, but to do our best to shut down the actual feeling of those emotions. When a child throws a tantrum and kicks another kid, we haven't traditionally been very good about explaining that the anger they're feeling is OK, and that it's just the display of anger (the kicking) that's not very constructive. Instead, we were usually taught that the anger itself was a bad thing and we should control it. Hell, not even positive emotions are safe. Excessive displays of joy are also shut down. A child's squeals of laughter or excited plea for someone to come and share their enthusiasm are often met with commands to 'keep it down!' by tired and weary adults. Back in my corporate life, I was even once told that I was going to ruin my chances of being promoted to an executive management position because I was deemed too happy, and was advised to become more serious and sombre at work (because obviously, happiness equals immaturity.). We've done our best not only to diminish displays of emotions, but to get rid of the feelings themselves.

This reluctance to engage with our emotions has done more to keep us stuck in our limiting beliefs than anything else. What's worse, it's all based on a misunderstanding. You see negative emotions in their natural state don't actually feel the way most people think they do. Natural fear, for example, feels much more like reluctance than anxiety (except for life-threatening fear, of course). Natural anger is a quick rush of energy that most people would see as frustration. Natural sadness lasts a few minutes and would, by most people's standards, be defined as feeling slightly down. What most people understand when they think of anger, fear, depression and the like, is actually the result of *severely repressed* negative emotion. Anger that has been stewing for years or even generations feels very different from natural anger. It turns into blind rage and murderous hatred. Sadness that has never been allowed to shift feels heavy and dark and hopeless. It turns into severe depression. Fear that has been allowed to be a constant companion, turns into panic attacks, anxiety and paranoia. The main reason that we're so afraid of our negative emotions is that they've become so volatile, and yet the reason they've become so volatile is because we're afraid of our emotions.

When you put a pressure cooker on the stove and turn the heat up, you're going to need to release the pressure every once in a while, or it will, eventually, explode. In other words, you either let the pressure out voluntarily, in a controlled fashion, or it will erupt in an uncontrolled way. Our negative emotions are just the same. When we don't allow this natural progression to take its course, we let the pressure build. It then explodes out of us in an uncontrolled fashion, and usually at the most inconvenient moment. This is when we go off on the poor waitress who didn't do anything to deserve our rage. This is when we break down at work and have to run to the bathroom to cry. This is when we turn into 'crazy bitches' and stalk the hottie from the office. All of these types of volatile reactions and behaviours are uncontrolled eruptions of suppressed emotion.

This is an important point to understand. If you're afraid of your negative emotions, you can't work with them, you can't hear the message that they have for you. If you're a healer who is afraid of negative emotions, you won't be able to help others, as you'll try to lead them away from their emotional responses, judging them to be too ugly or scary. If you're a parent who is afraid of negative emotions, you'll teach your kids to suppress them just like you learnt to do. If you want to break the cycle and truly shift to the positive side of the Spectrum, you'll have to stop looking at negative emotions as a bad thing, and see them for the helpful messengers they are.

Chapter 8
Understanding Our Emotions

Our emotions, all of them, are simply messengers, letting us know whether what we're currently focusing on, and therefore what we are bringing into our realities in greater and greater fashion, is what we actually want or not. In fact, our emotions are our first feedback – without which we have no way of knowing what we're really focusing on. If we know how to decrypt our emotions, if we know how to receive and understand the messages they contain, we'll be able to use that information to move up the Spectrum easily and quickly, feel better, and set up Progressions of Manifestations that will fill our realities with experiences and stuff that we actually want.

In order to understand the messages our emotions contain, we'll be dissecting which belief systems trigger which emotion. In other words, we'll be mapping different belief systems to different parts of the Spectrum, a process that will help you fully understand why we humans feel, react and act the way we do.

Beliefs systems of the seven emotional groups

You've already been introduced to the basic emotional groups in the Spectrum of Empowerment in Chapter 7, so now let's build on that structure and look at the beliefs of each of the emotional groups.

Belief systems of emotional group 1: DEPRESSION

- **Emotions:** Deep depression, total despair, total powerlessness

- **Spectrum location**: Lowest point on the Spectrum; it doesn't get any worse than this.

- **Level of empowerment:** None. The world is a horrible, painful place and there's nothing anyone can do.

At this end of the Spectrum, we feel completely powerless: running back and forth in our pit, having been surrounded by unfulfilled and rotting desires for a long, long time. There's very little life energy flowing, no fun, no joy, no enthusiasm. In fact, those emotions, and any thoughts that accompany them, are totally inaccessible at this point.

This is where the clinically depressed hang out, as well as those who are addicted to drugs (when they are crashing). They don't tend to interact much with society, as they usually hide themselves away. Since the world at this end of the Spectrum is a dark and hostile place, other people represent nothing but more pain and disappointment. Notice that even if the person knows this is not logically true, the feelings can still persist. Life is meaningless (it's all just shit), and nothing makes any sense. There's no hope, no way out and no one can help.

The value of these dark, heavy emotions is in their pain. While the same can be said in a general sense about all negative emotions, it applies exponentially to group 1. Stay here long enough, and you'll do anything to get out. While the Spectrum theoretically goes to infinity in both directions (there's no limit to how awesome or bad things can get), it *is* actually limited on the 'negative' side by our own ability and willingness to handle pain. Each of us has a limit and when we reach it, we make a change. This is what people refer to as hitting rock bottom – our breaking point – and sometimes we have to hit it more than once before we'll really do something about it (just as I was driven to the brink of a breakdown by my workaholism *several times…*). I call this the 'Breaking Point Method of Growth', and it's employed by almost everyone (it's our current default method of growth).

Imagine that you've heard of this awesome party, and you want to go. Someone's given you directions and you head off the way you've been told to go. Only, after just a little while, you get a weird feeling. You're not sure that you're going the right way. But you check your directions and according to them, you're right on track. The party is supposed to be in this amazing neighbourhood, in a house with a huge garden and pool and tennis courts and ponies. And a chocolate fountain you can swim in – and another to feast on… *Obviously*. But as you keep on walking down the road, the neighbourhood just keeps getting worse. It begins to smell awful; there's graffiti everywhere; there's trash in the street; all the cars are on blocks; that guy on the corner just flashed some drugs at you and a knife, and what you're pretty sure is his poop jar; is that a dead body over there? You begin to get more and more uneasy. You check your directions again, but, yep, you're still on the right track. Now, a few hoodlums come out of an alley, and after they snap their fingers to a catchy tune (this is how I imagine all groups of hoodlums – thank you *West Side Story*), they being to harass you and shove you around. You're really scared now, but the party *has* to be around here somewhere, right? I mean, the directions said so! The hoodlums start to smack you around and one of them has a baseball bat. They begin to beat the crap out of you. You think you just saw one of your teeth fly across the street. And yet still, you persist.

Now, let me ask you something: how long will it take before you come to your senses and get the hell out of there? How much pain will you bear before you consider the idea that maybe, just maybe the stupid directions were wrong, and your gut feeling that you were going the wrong way was actually true? How difficult does it have to be before you give up and walk away? Of course, as long as you take this analogy literally, your answer would probably be 'I would've gotten the hell out of that neighbourhood well before things got really ugly.' But when you apply this metaphor to your life, when the party you're looking for is monetary success or love, and the directions someone gave you are your limiting beliefs, you'll realize that you're actually willing to put up with a whole lot of pain.

How long have you stayed in a job you hated? How far past its expiration date was your last relationship before you finally cut your losses (or they were cut for you)? How much pain did it take to bring you down? Are you actually proud of the fact that nothing short of a serious illness will cause you to take a day off? Would you rather nearly break under the workload of doing everything yourself, than ask someone for help? If you're like most people alive today, you won't get up and walk out of that neighbourhood until you absolutely can't take it any more – when you've hit your breaking point.

This is why people stay in a job they hate until they get fired, rather than quit. This is why relationships often have to get really ugly before people break up. This is why we often have to get ill before we're willing to do anything about the chronic stress in our lives. When it becomes too painful to stay in the wrong neighbourhood, we have to get out. But we're often unwilling to move until that day arrives. This method of growth isn't 'wrong'. It's actually served us quite well. You see you don't have to understand the information in this book in order to let go of resistance and keep raising your energy. That process will happen automatically (you can't stop having experiences that will create more desires, and sooner or later you will realize those desires, because not doing so will simply become too painful). Knowing about Deliberate Receiving gives you a shortcut. Growing via the Breaking Point Method is slow and, well, *painful*. If you want to stop taking detours into the wrong neighbourhoods and just go straight to the party, you'll want to learn how to trust that little voice that told you right away that you were heading in the wrong direction. You'll want to pay attention to how you feel.

The Breaking Point Method of Growth entails waiting until a situation becomes so painful that it forces us to make a change for the better.

Ignoring those feelings to the degree that you become totally numb, essentially allowing the hoodlums to beat you up in perpetuity, stems from a feeling of total powerlessness, which evokes a state of depression. Depression goes beyond sadness. There's a feeling of detachment, of almost not being alive and no longer caring if you continue to live (for many, death actually feels like a welcome release). This state is the result of years (sometimes generations) of powerlessness, staying in a situation that's incredibly painful and not doing anything about it.

I want to make it clear that I'm not, in any way, diminishing what those with depression endure. Nor am I saying that it's all their fault and that all they'd have to do is to get off their butts and change their situation. That's the whole heart of the problem: in depression, we wouldn't even have access to the idea that we could do that! The limiting belief system at the heart of depression states that life is not only ugly and horrible (so, pain is to be expected), but there's nothing that can be done about it. So anyone at this level would go out into the world and just absorb all the hits, just take them. They wouldn't stand up for themselves. They also wouldn't change anything in their lives (what's the point?). They will not talk it out or seek to feel better or try to get help. All of those behaviours require at least a smidgen of the belief that feeling better is possible.

The good news is that this state is not sustainable (it's simply too painful) and no one stays at the same level of depression for long. We'll eventually get so sick of being in pain that we'll attempt to do something about it. This isn't generally a conscious decision, as much as the survival mechanism kicking in. The pressure will become so great that we'll either have to do something voluntarily, or have an uncontrolled release (I believe the official term for this is 'freaking out'). The bad news is that this freak-out, in its most extreme form, can come in the form of suicide or attempted suicide (as a way to escape the pain). In a less extreme form, we will move up the Spectrum but can fail to come all the way out of DEPRESSION, due to a resistance to the emotions we'd then feel, causing us to slide right back down. In this way, it's possible to become trapped in DEPRESSION (or a cycle between ANGER and DEPRESSION) for years.

I'll explain this 'cycle of doom', as I like to call it, as well as how to escape it once and for all, in Chapter 11.

Belief systems of emotional group 2: SHAME

- **Emotions:** Guilt, shame, severe insecurity, unworthiness, self-blame, fake gratitude, resentment

- **Spectrum location:** Between DEPRESSION and ANGER

- **Level of empowerment:** The power lies with some outside source (God, other people) who loves me, but will not show that love until I prove myself worthy, which I am not and can never be. I should be grateful for any scraps I do receive, and if I don't get any, which I generally don't, it's clearly my own fault.

When you experience emotions in the SHAME group, the world is still a dark and hostile place, but it's not completely random. How and when pain is doled out can be controlled to a degree, by appeasing some outside source. This is where self-blame lives: where you take responsibility for everything, even if it's not within your control. You feel you should anticipate everyone's needs and cater to them and feel horrible when anything goes wrong.

This is also where you put everyone ahead of yourself: you're not just *not first*, you're dead last, or not even on the roster. You are not important. All that matters is that everyone else is happy. That's the only way to stay safe (by appeasing others, we can exercise a small amount of control over when and how much pain comes our way). Whatever bad thing happens to you, you must've deserved it. It's always your own fault. Always.

The value in these emotions is that they allow us to feel safer than in total powerlessness. We're essentially trading service to others for permission to feel good – if we please everyone else and they are happy, we will be safe. This is like making a deal with the hoodlums; you'll live in the hood with them and will do all their cooking, cleaning and drug running and they won't kill you (they'll still beat you up from time to time, but not as badly). You're striking a bargain, one that allows you to feel more secure.

The belief system that causes the emotions in DEPRESSION is one that states that you have no real value outside of what you can do for others. This is a step above DEPRESSION, because they don't feel they have any value at all. The depressed person has no control whatsoever over the pain that's inflicted upon them, while the ashamed person can exercise a modicum of control by pleasing others. They might even sometimes get some positive feedback, if they've done their job well (the depressed person, by comparison, won't perceive any positives at all).

Of course, it's impossible to really please others, especially if they're not already happy. No one can manifest in someone else's reality. No one can actually change the vibration of another person. We can influence them, but they'll still have to allow themselves to be influenced (see the Resources section for a bonus article that will explain exactly how this works). Someone might decide that they'll feel better if you do their bidding, and they will actually feel slightly better for a little while, although not because of what you did for them. People who need others to please them aren't exactly in a high vibration themselves. In fact, they're usually stuck somewhere in the upper register of SHAME or ANGER, where people gain their power by manipulating others. So, this person that you're pleasing will temporarily feel better because they were able to exercise power over you, not because what you did actually made them happy. Keep in mind that none of this is usually done consciously. The person doing the manipulating will generally believe that if they get whatever it is they asked you for, they will genuinely feel better. And, like I said, they do. Just not for very long. That's when the next request or demand comes...

A person stuck in this group has accepted their situation and will often take pride in their martyrdom. They will even hoist some help upon others in an effort to feel better, even when those others aren't even asking for help. Think of your grandma, insisting that you have another helping of her delicious food, even when you're so full that you can't breathe. In that moment, your grandma is actually manipulating you so she can feel better (she feels worthy through service, whether the service is asked for or not). If you allow her to guilt you into doing her bidding, you've slipped into SHAME.

As you can see, you don't have to be 'stuck' in a group in order to experience the emotions within it. In fact, on some issues, and with certain people, you're bound to dip into SHAME from time to time (if you ever feel guilty about anything, you've met this group – which, and this has to be said, would be the worst and yet most accurate name for a sleazy consulting firm ever). You can, for example, feel unworthy when it comes to one specific area of your life, but not in any other area. I once told a friend of mine that she clearly had an insecurity (she had asked me to help her, and so I read her energy), only to have her give me an appalled look and inform me that she didn't have an insecure bone in her body. And of course, she didn't. Except the one, that is, which she did end up discovering once she was fully ready. Until that point, however, my words held no meaning for her. It's important to understand that this is not an all-or-nothing game. You're never just sitting on one point of the Spectrum. Different issues within you will evoke different emotions, and therefore be tied to different beliefs.

When we are experiencing the SHAME group, we are basically saying that the needs and wants of others, no matter how trivial by the way, are more important than our own needs and wants. Someone in the lower Spectrum of SHAME and guilt will choose to do the most meaningless of tasks for someone else over the most important task for themselves (like running to get you coffee over being on time for their very important doctor's appointment).

Belief systems of emotional group 3: ANGER

- **Emotions:** Blame (blaming others), anger, revenge, hatred, rage, jealousy

- **Spectrum location:** Between SHAME and FRUSTRATION

- **Level of empowerment:** The power lies with an outside source that doles out both bad AND good, so both are theoretically possible. This power source plays favourites, however, so some people are unfairly privileged. We have the ability to 'earn' favours with hard work or by proving ourselves valuable or by paying a price, but the game is still rigged against us (meaning, we lose more than we win).

The emotions in ANGER represent the first hint of actual empowerment. Whereas in SHAME, all the power lies with an outside source, which must be appeased and may then throw us a few scraps, in anger one can work hard to try and tip the unfair balance back a little.

Anger is the emotion that takes us out of powerlessness. When you've had enough of the hoodlums beating you up, of allowing them to use and abuse you, you'll stand up and fight back. You'll scream, 'No more!' And you'll, at the very least, run away. By removing yourself from the situation, you're withdrawing your permission for them to beat you up. You stop subjecting yourself to the situation that's causing you pain. This is generally the best-case scenario. The worst-case scenarios happen when destructive, uncontrolled anger explodes forth, after the pressure has been allowed to build for too long. This is when people lash out at others, either verbally or physically. This is when rage and the need for revenge lead to manslaughter and murder. But before you get scared of anger (or more scared than you already are), let me remind you that this type of expression of anger isn't actually anger; it's *suppressed* anger. If you want to avoid these kinds of outbursts, you'll need to make friends with it and embrace it, instead of running away from it. My point?

**Fighting back is more empowering
than sitting there and taking it.**

In order to stand up and shout, 'No!' and run away, or even fight back, you have to believe that whatever life is about (and you may still not know what that is), it simply can't be about getting beaten up and just taking it. It can't be about being used and abused. It can't always be about the needs of others. This belief system requires you to ask, 'What about me for a change?' And THAT point of view requires you, for the first time on the Spectrum, to actually value yourself.

When you first enter into any kind of real empowerment, you begin to say things like 'I don't deserve to be treated this badly!' and 'This shit isn't right!' You have the realization that you just can't take it any more, and that you're simply not going to put up with your situation any longer, screw the consequences. In fact, one of the beneficial properties of anger is that we stop caring so much about how others will be affected (this is not detrimental when anger is released constructively, as I'm about to show you).

You see, when you care 100 per cent about other people's feelings and 0 per cent about your own, you will never do anything that's good for you until everyone in your environment agrees. And while those who need you to put their needs above your own are surrounding you, you will never get their agreement. In fact, you won't have attracted any other kind of people from a powerless state, since they wouldn't mirror back your own propensity to put them first. Another powerless person in shame and guilt would be doing what you're doing – trying to give you all their power, while you're trying to give them yours. You'd only end up fighting over who gets to put the other first ('No, YOUR needs come first!' 'No, YOUR needs come first!'). The mirror to someone who gives away all their power in order to feel good is someone who needs to take power from others so they can feel good.

When you give away ALL of your power (DEPRESSION), you'll never do anything for yourself. In the SHAME group, you begin to value yourself a little more. You don't ask for anything, of course, but you learn subtle (and not so subtle) ways of manipulating others around you into doing you favours. At the bottom end of the Spectrum, just to the right of DEPRESSION, these manipulations will be mostly about survival – you appease others so that you can continue to exist. This is, incidentally, where people in abusive relationships usually hang out. In the higher part of the SHAME group, you begin actively to manipulate others in order to get not only what you need to survive, but also some of what you want. As you move higher up the Spectrum, these feelings of deserving turn into anger. At this point, you actually start placing your own needs above those of others; you begin to take care of yourself.

It's at this point that I tend to lose people a little. A lot of you will have read that last passage and bristled at the idea of putting your own needs above those of others. After all, isn't that why we're in the mess we're in today? Isn't this the height of selfishness and isn't selfishness the root of all evil? No, no and straight up, no. Here's where the explanation of the Spectrum comes in handy. You see, putting your own needs ahead of everyone else's doesn't mean that you stop caring about others. It doesn't mean that you now have to walk over bodies to get what you want, become a heartless bastard, take ice cream from children and kick puppies. Serving others from a place of powerlessness is very different from serving others from a place of empowerment. In other words, an activity performed in the lower part of the Spectrum will be very different from that same activity performed in the upper part of the Spectrum. You can't ever truly give to anyone if you're not giving to yourself first.

Think of one of those big, round fountains you can find in old town squares, especially in Southern Europe. The water spurts out of the top and fills up the highest reservoir. It then trickles down into the next largest reservoir and so on until it fills the basin at the very bottom. People who want to drink from the fountain take the water from the bottom reservoir. The fountain continuously fills itself up and then gives and gives and gives from the overflow. If the fountain tried to give people water before filling up those reservoirs, they would never get filled. It would run dry. When you take care of yourself first, you have so much more to give others, but without becoming depleted.

Remember that self-care is not the same as selfishness.

Although, when you shift from SHAME into ANGER, it's important that you allow yourself temporarily to be a bit more selfish in the name of self-care. It means being willing to stand up for yourself and stop the unhealthy giving you've been practising for so long. It can often mean severing relationships and walking away from people who gain their power from using and abusing you. This isn't about slinking off into the night to lick your wounds, only to have them inflicted upon you again the next day. This is about stomping off in broad daylight, spitting defiantly and kicking up dirt, so that all may know *they can no longer fuck with you*.

Anger is also about taking all that blame you've been placing on yourself and pushing it outwards, onto others. Again, I know that many of you will bristle at this idea, but hear me out. We're still working in the lower part of the Spectrum at this point, so we're still powerless to a degree. In total powerlessness or DEPRESSION, we see the power as lying with an outside source. In SHAME, we hope to get some scraps from that power, even if we don't deserve them. In ANGER, we begin to demand that some power be given to us. And, in order to do that, we have to have someone of whom we can make those demands. Someone or something has to represent the power structure if it isn't within us. Whereas in the lowest end of the Spectrum we want to appease this power structure, in ANGER, as we move more into empowerment, we begin to demand more justice, more fairness. We want the power to be distributed more evenly. The higher you climb on the Spectrum, the fairer the world becomes.

In moving into ANGER, we still believe that someone else has what we want (they have the power), but we no longer believe that they're more deserving of our stuff than we are. We begin to believe that if they have more power than we do, it's due to some kind of error. It's unfair. This is not the way it's supposed to be. We shift the blame. Instead of our pain being our own fault (it's just because we're so unworthy), we see it as being *their* fault: 'them' being whomever we're assigning the power to, be it our boss, neighbour, the government, the 1 per cent, corporations, those who disagree with us, etc. And this is perfectly natural. There's nothing wrong with blaming others, as long as you do so constructively and don't get stuck in that emotional state. Of course we've all seen the angry grumps at the bar, bitching about whose fault it is that they are in the situation they're in, blaming the government or the other sports team for the fact that they're miserable. Does this look constructive? Does this look like healing to anyone? Of course not. These individuals are blaming others, but only to the degree that it makes them feel slightly better. They never allow themselves to move fully through the ANGER Spectrum and on up to the next group (FRUSTRATION). They're actually stuck in the cycle of doom, moving from DEPRESSION or SHAME to ANGER and back again, precisely because they never fully let their anger out. Like the pressure cooker that just goes off in order to release some steam, these individuals bitch and complain in order to release some of the pain, but never remove the cause of it. They never take the pot off the stove. Again, I'll explain exactly how to avoid this scenario in Chapter 11.

Those grumps at the bar may be displaying a type of destructive anger release, but they are demonstrating the natural progression of the Spectrum. When we are feeling powerless, we naturally and automatically move into ANGER. The key is to go from blaming yourself to blaming others and then taking responsibility. Responsibility and blame are not the same thing, which should become clear as I explain the upper range of the Spectrum. But you can't move through and past ANGER if you're unwilling to spend at least a little bit of time blaming others (in a constructive way, which I will show you how to do in Chapter 11 (*see page 206*). This natural propensity for blame is also why people in the lower part of the Spectrum become so easily offended. After all, it has to be someone's fault, and if it's not mine it has to be yours. When someone becomes defensive, when they do the equivalent of screaming, 'It's not *my* fault, it's *your* fault!' they're actually doing their best to move from SHAME to ANGER. They are empowering themselves. Again, most of the problems in our society are not due to people experiencing these emotions, but rather because they've become stuck in one of the lower emotional groups due to limiting beliefs, and have allowed the pressure to build. Let's not throw the baby out with the bath water; let's not demonize these emotions just because people often engage in exaggerated and destructive displays of those feelings.

You'll have seen anger in its natural state if you've ever watched a toddler playing with something he didn't have the dexterity for; joining two small building blocks, for example. The toddler wants to do something he can't do. He then feels a moment of powerlessness – something unwanted is happening and he can't do anything about it. He experiences a rush of anger and throws the building blocks down in frustration. He may even cry for a few seconds. But before you know it, he's moved on to something else, and is happily playing again. The building blocks have been forgotten.

This is what anger is supposed to look like. The toddler moved from powerlessness (he couldn't do something he wanted to do) to anger (a release of that powerlessness) easily and quickly, and then on up the Spectrum. The reason that anger usually doesn't look like that is because most people will not allow themselves to experience or express anger. So, it festers. We stay in a powerless state. We stay in the alley and let the hoodlums beat us up, while we get angrier and angrier and angrier. Finally, we explode and rip their faces off. Or yell at someone at the grocery store for seemingly no good reason. When we 'overreact' and anger comes flying out at an inopportune moment, it's always because we've kept ourselves imprisoned in a prolonged state of powerlessness ('I'm in a situation that I don't like and for whatever reason, I can't get out'), and the strain has become too much. That pressure cooker is going to blow, eventually. It has to.

As always, this can be observed on an individual level, as well as a collective one. Have you ever noticed that people in our society are really, really angry? Generations of powerlessness have created a pressurized situation that can't help but explode every once in a while. This doesn't solve the problem, but it does keep people from sinking into DEPRESSION. Even *some* anger will help to keep us from sliding down the Spectrum further.

Belief systems of emotional group 4: FRUSTRATION

- **Emotions:** Frustration, discouragement, pessimism

- **Spectrum location:** Between ANGER and HOPE

- **Level of empowerment:** The power lies with some outside source, and it is actually a fair one (more like a machine), we just have to figure out how it works. If we can crack the code, we can get what we want (or at least something in that direction).

This is the last level of powerlessness before we cross the threshold. Getting something wanted is possible, but it comes at some kind of price. If we can figure out what the price is and pay it, we can prosper.

In the FRUSTRATION group, we feel that we're close; what we want is just out of reach, like something we can see behind a glass window. This is usually the point at which we'll try *everything*. We're pretty sure that we can get what we want, and we've moved past SHAME and ANGER, for the most part. We've walked away from the hoodlums and have begun to make our way out of the nasty neighbourhood. Things are looking up and we can observe them getting better. Most of the pain has gone (we're nearly at the neutral point) and we're eager to experience pleasure; we know it's out there, but we just don't quite know how to get it.

There's actually quite a bit of empowerment at this level – you believe, at least to some degree, that you can and should get what you want, you're just not yet sure that you actually *will*. When compared to the DEPRESSION, SHAME and ANGER belief systems, this one seems downright swimming in empowerment, which is why so many people accept this as the last stage before they're 'done'. And, if the goal was to simply become pain-free, to get to the Zero Point, they'd be right. Only, zero isn't as good as it can get. And deep down, we know that, which is why we feel so frustrated when we get close to that threshold. We feel the pressure to cross it. This is the first time in the Spectrum that we can experience positive pressure – although most people won't interpret it that way. This is the feeling you get just before you do something really big (like bungee jump off a bridge). You're scared, but you really, really want to have this experience. Our innate knowledge of what's on the other side of that Spectrum (empowerment) pulls us towards it, but our remaining resistance is still blocking us. Again, it's like looking through a glass window; we're so close we can practically taste what we want, but it's just out of reach.

Feelings of frustration come about when we're pretty sure that we *can* get what we want, but don't yet totally believe that we *will*. We make statements such as 'I don't know… maybe… I mean it's got to be possible, right? But how? Arrrrrgh!' As we entertain our doubts, we feel frustration. Keep in mind that the amount of time you spend in each emotional group is a very individual thing. It will vary not only from person to person, but also from situation to situation. Someone who's just had a huge anger release, for example, could blow right past FRUSTRATION and even the Zero Point (neutral) and swoosh immediately up the Spectrum into HOPE, or even ENTHUSIASM. When you effectively block your own, powerful energy from flowing, the pressure will build behind that blockage. When you bust through the dam, which is what a release of anger is, when you break through the blockage, the energy that's been stuck behind it will flow. The more energy you've suppressed, the faster it will flow. So, someone who's been in misery for a long time can actually be catapulted forward quite rapidly as soon as they change their limiting beliefs.

Others will go through each stage at a slower pace, exploring each one thoroughly before moving on. And while neither is wrong, you can speed up your progress considerably by understanding the Spectrum and deliberately shifting your emotions.

Zero Point: the Void

- **Emotions:** Seeming lack of emotion, feeling numb

- **Spectrum location:** Zero Point, smack dab in the middle

While the Zero Point isn't technically an emotional group, it is a stage that deserves a mention, especially because it does have the tendency to freak people out. You see, when you move from the lower part of the Spectrum to the upper one, you move from a pain-motivated way of living to a pleasure-motivated way of living. In other words, you stop doing all the stuff that hurts you, and start doing the stuff that actually feels good. But, in order to make that shift, we have to be willing to let our pain receptors recover and switch over to become pleasure receptors.

Imagine that you've been spending the last couple of minutes pounding on your thumb with a hammer. You've given your poor thumb some pretty good whacks and it's red and sore and in a lot of pain. Now imagine that you stop doing that, and instead, you begin to caress your thumb with a feather. Do you think that feather would actually feel good, or do you think your thumb would need a little time to recover before you could feel such a subtle caress? Of course, it's the second one. A callus doesn't form from something purely pleasurable. It forms because of something that's irritating or damaging. The callus doesn't just numb out the irritation and pain, though, it also numbs out potential pleasure. When the irritation stops, the callus has to be allowed to heal before the more sensitive pleasure receptors can do their job.

This area of the Spectrum is what I call 'the Void'. It can feel like numbness, like total lack of emotion, like you're floating. It's not bad or painful, it's just a kind of blah, nothing feeling, which is precisely what causes people to freak out. They mistake this numbness for the numbness that comes from severely repressed anger. They wrongly interpret the blah and listless feeling as the unmotivated state of depression. But DEPRESSION and the Void aren't anywhere near each other on the Spectrum. There is pain in DEPRESSION. There is no pain in the Void. Misinterpreting the numbness of the Void as a bad thing (instead of a holiday from pain), however, can cause us to slide right back down the Spectrum. The thought that something has gone wrong is always a powerless one.

You can find yourself in the Void anytime you've let go of a painful belief – anytime you've stopped hitting yourself with the hammer. But don't despair. Like I said, nothing has gone wrong. You're simply taking a breather, a break from feeling bad. This seeming lack of momentum – nothing much seems to be happening, which can feel boring – is also a great time to make the massive shift of changing your focus from one of pain minimization to pleasure maximization. It's a lot easier to change your direction when you're standing still (or moving very slowly) than when you're rushing in the opposite direction as fast as you can. The value of the Void is that it's a great opportunity to focus differently to how you have been doing. It's also the perfect time to rest and recover from all the damage that the resistance did – to let your thumb heal now that you've stopped pounding it with a hammer.

Belief systems of emotional group 5: HOPE

- **Emotions:** Hope, optimism, contentment, gratitude

- **Spectrum location:** Between FRUSTRATION and ENTHUSIASM

- **Level of empowerment:** The power still lies with some outside source (like the Universe or God), but it's doled out fairly. There's a system, and we believe that we can and will figure it out.

This is the first level of empowerment, after crossing the Zero Point threshold. Getting something we want is not only possible, it happens frequently (we have examples!) and there's no price. It's no longer about deserving or being worthy, because we know (at least to some degree) that we are. Things are going to be OK, even if we're not yet sure how.

The HOPE group is basically the opposite of the FRUSTRATION group. Whereas in FRUSTRATION, you believe that it's *possible* to get what you want, in HOPE, you actually begin to believe that you *will*. This is when you actively begin to look forward to your future (the future is bright). This is when you feel optimistic. You have a feeling that good things are coming your way. You may still have doubts, but you spend more time thinking of how things will work out than fearing that they won't.

The only danger in this group is that we tend to settle for it, having believed for years that the goal was simply to get to the Zero Point. Once we experience some actual pleasure, we can become afraid of losing that pleasure and sliding back down the Spectrum. A fear of pain can actually cause us to revert to a painful state. This is where an understanding of the Spectrum and how things manifest can come in super handy. If you know what causes you to slide up and down that Spectrum, then it is within your control; you can't and won't be afraid that such a downward slide will simply happen randomly. In other words, once you cross the threshold, the world is no longer a random place. Bad stuff doesn't just happen to you any more, it comes as a result of something you have control over – your focus. And instead of *blaming* yourself for having manifested something unwanted, you take *responsibility* for your focus and simply change it.

This is why blame and responsibility aren't even close to the same thing, even though people stuck in the lower part of the Spectrum will perceive them to be (when they hear 'it's your responsibility', they hear 'it's your fault').

> **Blame is the emotion you feel when you're trying to take control from a place of powerlessness. Responsibility is taking control from a place of empowerment.**

When you take responsibility, you believe that you will actually get the outcome you want. When you blame, you're merely trying to avoid the outcome you don't want. Remember that in this part of the Spectrum, we're no longer focused on minimizing pain, but on maximizing pleasure.

Belief systems of emotional group 6: ENTHUSIASM

- **Emotions:** Enthusiasm, positive expectation, appreciation

- **Spectrum location:** Between HOPE and JOY

- **Level of empowerment:** The power lies within me, and I am helped by a benevolent outside source (God, the Universe). I am able to attract anything I want.

The emotions in the ENTHUSIASM group represent a knowledge that things are always working out. Things are happening FOR you, not TO you. You will get what you want and you're looking forward to it.

In this emotional group, you begin to see yourself as the centre of the power, while the Universe, or God, or other people help you out. It's a much more collaborative effort. Whereas in HOPE, you tend to say things like 'stuff always happens for a reason', while still thinking, at least to some degree, that this reason is determined by someone outside of yourself (albeit a benevolent force), in ENTHUSIASM you start to understand that it really is a mechanical construct, and you are fully in charge of getting what you want. Things do happen for a reason, and it's always a good one, one that serves you, one that gets you closer to what you want. You are in charge of determining what you want and you will get it.

Whereas in HOPE, you're beginning to believe that you will get what you want, in ENTHUSIASM you expect to. You understand that even when something manifests that seems to be unwanted, it's only there as a messenger, there to move you in a direction you've been resisting, but a direction in which you want to go. This is where your dreams become really fun, even and especially the big ones. You no longer worry too much about being realistic, about dreaming within your limitations. You allow your imagination to run wild, to bring you visions of playing a much, much bigger role than anything you've imagined before.

This is precisely why people often get scared and slide back down the Spectrum, however. When we get a glimpse of just how powerful, spectacular and grand we are, it can shake us up. Sure, we may not be totally powerless any more (we've moved on from that), but can we really be this awesome? Can we really have lives filled not just with contentment, but also with bliss? This is where most of us find out just how uncomfortable dreaming big can be. This is also where fears of being labelled as (or actually being) crazy, or having delusions of grandeur come in. But think of this: the only difference between someone shouting, 'I'm going to be president!' being shunned as a nutcase or embraced as a visionary, is whether or not that person actually becomes president. We're so quick to shut down anyone with a big dream. Until they make it. Then, suddenly, we knew all along that they were something special.

Everyone who ever changed the world in their own way, everyone who ever accomplished huge dreams had to, at one point in their lives, make the decision to stop caring completely about what others thought, and just go for it. It's in the ENTHUSIASM group that we become truly free. We no longer live our lives for others, but fully for ourselves. We understand that we will benefit the world much more by focusing on our own joy, on living our own big dreams and by inspiring others to their own full empowerment, than by keeping ourselves small.

This is also where we begin to see solutions everywhere. We see the economy changing for the better (not just recovering, but morphing into a whole, new and improved system). We see the innovation, the inventions, the technology that's fuelling faster and faster evolution, we become aware of all the people in the world who already get it, who are already working towards a brighter future. We see the kindness and the joy that's rampant, and we celebrate it. We see the rebellion that's taking our society out of powerlessness, and we celebrate that, too. We understand and perceive that the world is getting better and better and we begin to see how we can participate fully in that evolution. We begin to understand why we're really here.

Belief systems of emotional group 7: JOY

- **Emotions:** Love, passion, joy, full empowerment, celebration

- **Spectrum location:** At the very top, from where it just gets better and better and better to infinity.

- **Level of empowerment:** Fully empowered: the power lies within me and the Universe is my mechanical servant. I am the power, the Universe, God, etc. I am ALL THAT IS. I am the game and the player.

At this level of empowerment, there is no doubt whatsoever that you will get what you want. You trust completely that everything will always work out, and you relax into that knowledge, content just to the wave of awesomeness. You have no need to control anything. The process of realizing your newly spawned desires has been fully automated and you simply go with the flow, enjoying each and every moment (in the NOW) as fully as possible.

Before I explain full empowerment to the best of my ability (this is where words really start to fail us), let me reiterate that this is a Spectrum, and no part of the Spectrum is bad or good. There is only what we prefer and what we don't prefer, what we want, and what we don't want. Being in JOY is not objectively better than being in DEPRESSION, it's just another destination on the Spectrum, and one that you might want to choose. But because this is a Progression, you can't continuously stay in JOY. The second you make it to that 'destination', you'll spawn another desire. You'll identify some way to make it even better, not because you're dissatisfied with where you are, but because you're always striving for more awesomeness.

Let's say that you become a master at something, like playing tennis. You practise every day and observe your improvement. That makes you feel happy. Then, you start to win matches. That makes you happy. Then, you go up against tougher and tougher opponents, and so on. No matter what level you accomplish, you keep looking for the next challenge. You want to play against more skilled athletes, play matches in front of bigger crowds and for bigger prizes. You may even seek out extreme conditions to play in, such as the desert or high elevations, in order to create more challenges for yourself. If you run out of challenges in tennis, you might well start again with a new sport that excites you. The thing that brings you joy today will feel boring tomorrow.

Some people will read this and will want to argue that this doesn't sound joyful at all. It sounds more like running on a hamster wheel, never quite being satisfied with where you are. But this is a conclusion we would come to when holding a perspective from the lower end of the Spectrum. You see it only feels like a hamster wheel when you don't get what you want and don't believe that you will ever really get what you want. This is powerlessness. When you truly are getting what you want, and then get the next thing you want and so on, it doesn't feel like a hamster wheel at all. It feels more like being at an amusement park where you're enjoying the ride you're on and also looking forward to the next one. The difference between the hamster wheel and the amusement park is this: are you doing something you want to be doing as you move towards your next goal, or are you paying some kind of price?

In the JOY group, you completely and fully trust in the construct of the game, in your ability to get what you want and in the automated process that will deliver it to you. You no longer worry about anything; you simply go with the flow, *knowing* that everything that happens to you is taking you there. I call this state 'riding the wave'. It's like you're surfing a huge wave, one that you know you have the ability to stay on even if it's challenging, and your only work is to keep your balance and enjoy the ride. Of course, in order to relax fully and enjoy that ride, you can't be afraid of possibly falling off. This fear makes you slide right back down the Spectrum. It's based on the belief that falling off would be a bad thing (it's not), will be painful (it doesn't have to be) and that it will be difficult to get back on (it also doesn't have to be).

All of us have experienced this state of flow at some point in life. It's when we are so immersed in a joyful moment that we forget to worry about anything. These are often what we call the 'peak moments' of our lives; seeing your baby for the first time, the second you find out you got that huge promotion, falling in love, etc. These peak moments don't have to be few and far between. We can spend much more time in JOY than we currently do. But our goal should never be to spend 100 per cent of our time there. We have to allow for the dips, at least to some degree, in order to make our continued evolution possible. By noticing that the awesomeness has waned, we can determine what we'd now like to focus on to get to that awesome level again (and again, and again…). If we don't notice that the awesomeness has waned, it will continue to feel more and more boring, and will, eventually become painful, until we realize that we've stagnated and haven't allowed ourselves to move forwards. The good news is that when you spend most of your time in the upper end of the Spectrum, when you trust more in your ability to get what you want than the random horribleness of a powerless world, you won't dip into depression or huge displays of anger. You'll become more like that toddler, able to shift quickly and easily through the emotional Spectrum. With no more suppressed energy, you'll feel twinges of annoyance and frustration, instead of rage and depression. Your emotions will truly become your friends – valuable messengers that help you get what you want.

You may have noticed that I spent a great deal more time explaining the lower end of the Spectrum. There's a reason for this: people generally don't have any issues moving from an awesome life to an even more awesome one. Once you've climbed up the mountain and have gotten a better view, continuing that climb to an even better one isn't that hard. But when you're in the valley, when you're in the fog, when you haven't seen a solution in so long you've forgotten that they exist, that's when a tour guide can come in handy. When you're on the mountaintop, a map is interesting but not really necessary. When you're still looking for the mountain, a map can be a lifesaver.

Chapter 9

Awareness – What You Really Want and How You Actually Feel

Crossing the threshold into empowerment entails and requires becoming conscious of the fact that it's a game and we are in control of our holographic realities. We have to become aware of our focus, our feedback systems and our manifestations. This is easier said than done. Most people have no idea what they really want (oh, they often think they do, but they really don't) or how they really feel. Without this awareness, however, we can't become fully awake or fully empowered. We can't move out of the fog. So, if you are unaware, and I promise you that you are at least to some degree (we all are), how can you create that awareness? How can you notice something that you're not noticing? And what about if you are aware of your emotions to a degree, but have a habit of going with the worse-feeling option, anyway?

Becoming aware of how you feel

In the analogy of entering a bad neighbourhood and eventually meeting the finger-snapping hoodlums, you had a feeling of doubt when you first went down the wrong road, but intellectually overrode it. You checked the directions and decided in that moment to put more trust in the person who gave you the directions than your own gut. This is exactly how it is in the real world. You'll often have a bad feeling about something, an inkling that lets you know you're about to do something you really don't want to do – something that won't lead you to what you want, but you'll override it with your logical mind. Whenever you make that decision, you are ignoring the messenger. Do you have to go down that road in order to know that it really is the wrong way? Well, yes, you do. In order to gain the understanding that your gut was right all along, you'll have to have at least a few experiences where you can see a correlation between your emotions and the outcome. You felt bad right from the start and, low and behold, the situation really didn't work out well. Once you've had such an experience a few times, however, it is possible to see a pattern, and decide to trust that feeling. And many people *almost* do that! They exclaim 'I *knew* this was a bad idea!' when the shit hits the fan. You just knew that relationship or job wasn't going to work out. But if you knew that, then why did you go down that road anyway? The answer is threefold:

First, you trust more in the ugly road than the pretty one (hell, many of us can't even see the pretty one, because we don't believe it exists). So, it's a case of better the devil you know, because who's to say that the pretty road won't turn even uglier than the ugly road, eh? Weren't we taught to be careful what we wish for, to beware of the wolf in sheep's clothing and that everything comes at a price? Most people in the world today have been trained to put WAY more trust in the idea of things working out in the worst possible way than in the idea of things working out for the best. So, going down the familiar, painful road is actually the more comfortable choice.

In my very early twenties, I was on a double date with a friend. At the restaurant, my friend's date proceeded to place his hand firmly on my thigh and slide it in a decidedly naughty direction. My friend was sitting next to him while I was across the table, so this was clearly not a case of mistaken identity. I didn't want to make a scene, so I dragged my friend to the bathroom where I broke the uncomfortable news to her. Her response wasn't what I had expected (which was to dump the douchebag). She told me point blank, 'I believe you but I just have to see for myself, Melody. After all, he could be THE ONE.'

At the time, I didn't understand emotions and beliefs the way I do now, so I just thought she was an idiot. Now, I can look back on this event with a lot more compassion. My friend wasn't ready to let go of her belief of unworthiness and needed to keep going down the road of dating douchebags, even though she intellectually knew it wouldn't work out well. These were the only guys that would mirror back her low self-esteem (she was firmly stuck in the SHAME group) by seemingly needing her (fixing broken people is a way to serve others from a place of powerlessness), which allowed her to feel valuable. In her eyes, his straying hand actually represented a challenge. If she could now get him to choose her over me, it would prove her value to herself.

Note that even though my friend was not a stupid woman (despite what I thought at the time), and she even had a kind of intellectual understanding of what she was doing, her reaction was purely emotional. In fact, her emotional state caused her mind to come up with justifications for why she really had no choice but to go down that road. This is why we often react in ways that make no logical sense to us or others, why we engage in self-destructive behaviours and why we don't keep our New Year's resolutions. We simply don't trust that what we want (a non-douchey guy who treats us nice, for example) can come about, so we 'make do' with what we have.

The second reason that we choose the more painful road is that just about everyone carries the belief that pain or sacrifice is a good thing, as explained in the SHAME group (*see page 125*). We think that pain will actually lead us to something we want, which causes us *willingly* to choose the negative road. We know we're choosing a more painful path and that an easier way is available, but we figure any pain we experience now will be worth it later. This is the belief system that causes us to spend many horrible and torturous years in a job we hate, in the hope of then being rewarded for it at some later time, like in retirement or the afterlife. We trade suffering now for security later. Suffering and getting rewarded for it feels better to us than the idea of taking the easy way out and being punished for it later. We don't consider the idea that we could flourish now AND thrive later to be a valid one.

The third reason we keep going down a painful path rather than choose an easier one is, well, we're simply not aware that it's the more painful path. We have no idea how we really feel. Even when we later exclaim that we *knew* that this road wasn't going to work out for us, we really didn't have any awareness of it in the moment.

Hearing the messenger

By now you know that managing your vibration is the key to your manifested reality (getting the stuff you want), and your emotions are the key to your vibration. The emotion is the messenger, like a UPS delivery guy holding a package for you – a package containing the awareness of the limiting belief that's been holding you back. All you really have to do is open the door and accept the package, and you do that by engaging with the emotion – you have to actually *feel* it, something that we have unfortunately been taught not to do. When the message has been delivered, the messenger will go away. If you try to ignore the messenger, it will knock harder and harder and will, eventually, break down your door. In other words, the negative emotion will get stronger and stronger, and (unwanted) manifestations will come in that trigger this emotion in ever more volatile ways, until you finally pay attention and sign for the damn package already. These messengers take their jobs very seriously. Emotions aren't an intellectual construct, you are meant feel them. This is why you can't just think your way out of this; you have to be willing to get your emotional hands dirty.

When you ignore your negative emotions and larger manifestations (usually unknowingly), and this ignorance becomes automatic, you become unaware of how you're feeling. This usually happens when a belief, which contradicts what you want (limiting belief) has been with you for a long, long time, and you've become so used to the discomfort it causes that you're not even aware of it any more. This habitual unawareness is called 'denial'.

Denial is the act of unknowingly pretending to feel better than we actually do. In denial, we are not aware of how we are actually feeling.

Denial actually helps you to stay stuck in a limiting belief, since it masks how you're really feeling and therefore keeps you from being able to shift out of the emotional group you're in. The good news is that if you pay attention to how you feel, you can't be in denial. This is why emotional awareness is such a huge part of receiving the reality you want, even more so than understanding how the process works, which is incredibly helpful, but not strictly necessary – remember the toddler (*see page 133*)? If you could simply be completely aware of how you feel without judging those feelings, and therefore move in a direction that feels truly better, you'd be manifesting awesomeness in no time.

The sticking point here is that when you are in denial, you don't know it (and you don't want to know it). While being aware of how you feel will force you to move out of denial, many people (and yes, even those that have been studying inner work for a long time) *think* that they feel one way, but actually feel another. The key to breaking out of denial is to pay attention to how you feel, not an intellectual representation of how you *should* feel. You have to stop overthinking it. In order to be truly honest with yourself about how you're feeling, you have to be willing to actually experience your emotions.

This is why it's so important to accept that no part of the Spectrum is 'bad' (*see page 105*). If you demonize any part of the Spectrum, you will 'deny' any emotion you're not happy with.

The good news is that you can become aware of what's actually in your vibration (whether or not you're in denial about something) by looking at what's manifesting in your reality. You can pretend to feel better all you want, you can use pretty words, but you can't lie to the cosmic mirror because it will reflect your actual vibration back to you no matter what. If you think you're feeling pretty good, but your reality is filled with tons of crap you don't want, you're in denial. Don't worry; just about everyone is to some degree.

Think of denial as a kind of numbness to certain limiting beliefs, like a callus you've formed on your big toe so you won't feel the pebble in your shoe any more. This is a fine system, unless you go for a walk. When you engage in an activity that activates the irritating factor – in this cases the pebble rubbing against your toe, the point will come at which the denial (the callus) won't be enough any more. The pebble will eventually cause a blister, then a bigger blister that, if left unattended, will burst open and bleed and hurt and become infected and may even lead to the amputation of your foot. In other words, the problem (the unwanted manifestations) will get bigger and more painful, until you finally do something about it (like take the freaking pebble out of your shoe), or the situation kind of blows up and resolves itself (you go to the hospital and get your gangrenous foot chopped off).

If you're aware of how you feel, however, you'll notice the irritation from the pebble early on, and will be able to take it out of your shoe before any real damage is done. If you miss the initial irritation, you could still take note of that blister on your toe at the end of the day, search your shoe for a pebble and take it out. Our goal is always to find that pesky pebble as early as possible. So, even if you're in denial, meaning you don't feel the initial irritation, being aware of how you feel will, eventually, lead you to discover some evidence of your discomfort. And you don't have to wait until it's foot-chopping-off time, either.

Becoming aware of how you feel requires you to do three things:

1. **Make some space.** Distraction is denial's best friend. If you're constantly busy, you won't be able to 'hear' your messengers. You'll be so distracted that you won't have a chance to become aware of how you really feel. Take some time out to just sit and *feel*. Don't read, don't watch TV, don't eat, don't do anything. Just sit and feel. As little as 15 minutes a day of making space will make a huge difference. The more uncomfortable this exercise is for you, the more in denial you are.

2. **Embrace ALL emotions.** As long as you consider any emotional reaction to be inappropriate, you'll shut down the 'uglier' and more volatile ones, keeping you stuck in denial. It's not wrong to be angry with your kids. This doesn't make you a bad parent. It's not wrong to hate your parents. These are emotions that are telling you something, not reflections of what kind of person you are. Demonizing any emotion is the equivalent of barricading the door so the delivery guy can't

give you that message. Also, remember that your emotional reaction is always about you, not whoever triggered it. Your anger at your kids isn't about them. They were just the helpful angels that pointed it out to you by wrecking your freshly cleaned kitchen. So don't shy away from any emotion out of guilt. Embrace it and receive the message.

3. **Remember that your situation CAN change.** Often, we don't allow ourselves to acknowledge how we're really feeling because we don't think there's anything we can do to change our situation. After all, who wants to be aware of their gangrenous toe, if there's nothing they can do about the pain? If you believe there's no way you can get a better job, that all jobs are just as sucky, for example, then what's the point in acknowledging that you hate your job? Remind yourself that there are many options that you're not currently seeing. Also remember that just because you're not aware of the pain, that doesn't mean it's not affecting you negatively. Denial takes a lot of energy to maintain.

The key to your vibration

Hopefully by now you should be starting to understand how your emotional awareness is the key to becoming aware of your current vibration, *so that you can change it and manifest something else*. If you truly want to receive the reality you desire, if you want to change your life for the better, if you want to project a different frequency so your hologram can mirror back a different reality to you, you'll have to be willing to go the feeling route. Fortunately, this isn't actually hard. Why would it be? This feedback system is part of the game's design and the game is designed to be effortless.

Do you have trouble recognizing when you're hungry? Probably not. This is how easy it is to recognize how you're feeling. Now, you may have suppressed your hunger for so long that you no longer feel it until you get weak and shaky. But if you became just a little more aware, if you started looking for the early signs of hunger (in this case, signs of weakness), you'd be able to catch them earlier and earlier and the mechanism would come back. It's the same with your emotions.

You may not be aware of your emotional feedback at the earliest of stages (and even if you are, you probably don't trust it enough to base your decisions on it), but you are aware of what's currently not working in your life. You're aware of your manifestations and/or their absence. You'll either have manifested something that you don't like (someone yelling at you at work, for example), or you'll be aware of something that you want which is 'missing' from your reality (like not having a romantic partner when you really, really want one). You can use this information to manifest what you want, as soon as you figure out what that really is…

Becoming aware of what you want

In Chapter 4, I introduced you to the Progression of a Manifestation (*see page 48*), which showed how a manifestation goes from being a non-physical concept to being observable in your physical reality. Stage 1 of that Progression requires you to focus on what you want, but in order to do that you first have to figure out what that is. Now, I know that for many of you this will *seem* like a no-brainer. But you might be surprised to learn that most people actually fall off the proverbial horse at this stage. They either can't figure out what they want because they've only ever spent time identifying what they don't want, or they think they're focusing on WHAT they want, when they're actually focusing on HOW they think it has to come about.

Figuring out what you truly want isn't that hard when you understand the concepts of focus and progression (which you now do!), as well as the value of the unwanted (which you're about to).

One of the easiest ways to figure out what you want is first to figure out what you don't want. What are you complaining about? What do you not like about the situation you're in? Since most people have a much easier time and a hell of a lot more practice focusing on what they don't want than what they do, this step is usually incredibly easy. Identify what you've been bitching about and then use that to determine what you'd like instead.

This is actually the value of the unwanted stuff in your reality (also often called 'contrast', because it allows you to have *contrasting* experiences from which you can then choose). It's there to help you identify what it is that you want, spawning new desires. This unwanted crap you've been complaining about all your life is actually an integral and very necessary part of the game. Think of it this way: You're in your holographic room and it's completely empty. It's just a blank slate. You now want to create a fabulous piece of art from scratch. It could be anything, but it must be fabulous. Oh, and you can't revise it; whatever you come up with on your first try must meet the fabulous requirement. Go ahead, try and picture your piece of art now. It's not that easy, is it? Would you be able to come up with the exact version of what you want, from scratch? Or would you spend a lot of time staring blankly into the white room, paralysed by the infinite choices?

Now, imagine that there already was a piece of art in the room, one that you could turn into something fabulous. You have the ability to make changes, and you can keep on revising the art until you're satisfied. So, you see that it's kind of small, which allows you to decide that you'd like something bigger (and as you decide this, it just happens). The art is green, but you don't like green, so you decide to make it purple. It's a sculpture but you'd rather have a painting. You look at each characteristic and decide if you like it or not, and if not, what you'd like instead. In this way, your piece of art gets more and more fabulous (to you) over time. Are you beginning to see how the second scenario is much more efficient?

Designing reality from scratch is hard. There's simply too much choice. Changing a reality that's already there is far, far easier. When you have a starting point full of some stuff you like and some stuff you'd like to improve upon, and you can just keep on making improvements into perpetuity, creating the reality you want becomes a cinch. The unwanted stuff in your reality isn't just there to help you identify when you're focusing on what you don't want (by giving something unwanted to focus on). It's mainly there to help you figure out what you DO want, in ever-greater detail. Unwanted manifestations can be anything from something truly devastating in your reality to a detail that could be just a tad more awesome. All of it is there as a representation of what you're focusing on (even unknowingly), as well as to help you identify what you'd like to focus on instead. Let me repeat that in another, blunter way:

The unwanted crap in your reality is there to help you figure out what you want, and if you use it as such, it will go away. The only reason it ever sticks around and multiplies is because you insist on focusing on and bitching about it.

But, this is also why using what you don't want is the easiest way to start figuring out what you do want. It's actually designed to be that way. If, for example, you don't like your crappy, soul-sucking job, you could list all the reasons that you hate it. Let's list a few hypothetical examples:

- My boss is a giant butthead.

- He micromanages me.

- He yells at people.

- I feel unappreciated at work.

- My co-workers are idiots.

- I have no say in any decisions.

- The people at the top are idiots.

- My co-workers are also lazy.

- I get the most difficult clients.

- They make horrible demands that I can't meet.

So, you have a pretty specific-seeming list of what it is that you don't like about your job, which can help you figure out what you want instead. You can't just simply state the opposite of these manifestations, however. That won't get you very far. You could affirm, 'My boss is awesome! My co-workers are awesome! My clients are awesome!' all day long, but it wouldn't shift any energy at all. Why not?

You cannot shift your perspective from the unwanted to the wanted unless you back off and take a broader view. Remember the analogy with the telescope in Chapter 4 – you can't just swing that sucker around while focusing narrowly on the words on that computer screen. But, if you take a step back, look at the buildings and then find a different building before narrowing it down to a certain floor and window and desk, you'll find the target (frequency) you're looking for in no time. You can 'back off' in real life, by identifying the emotion that each one of these unwanted manifestations elicits from you and then finding the positive emotion you'd like to feel instead.

The statements in our list could come from several different emotional groups. For example, a person in DEPRESSION would make these statements from a place of total powerlessness, just accepting that this is how things are. A person in SHAME focuses on how everything was really their own fault ('my boss micromanages me because I make mistakes. My co-workers may be idiots, but it's really down to me to make it all work.') A person in ANGER would make these statements defiantly ('My boss micromanages me, but he has no reason to. I could be doing so much better if my co-workers and clients weren't idiots!'). Are you beginning to see why working strictly with words, without acknowledging the emotions they represent in each case, doesn't work? The words alone don't tell you where you are on the Spectrum.

For the sake of this example, let's say that you made this list from a place of ANGER. You're fed up with your job and you want out. You resent the hell out of your boss. You don't feel appreciated, you don't feel trusted and you don't feel successful (because you're not allowed to be). You've established how you really feel. Congratulations. Notice that in order to do that, you had to be honest about how you were feeling; you couldn't pretend it was 'fine', when it clearly wasn't. A lot of people who have been attempting to work with the Law of Attraction deliberately, will make the mistake of trying to feel better about a situation without first figuring out what their current emotional state is. So, they make a list of all the positive qualities of their boss and co-workers before they've acknowledged what's actually bothering them. Can this work? Yes, *IF* this technique was the right one for where the person was on the Spectrum. But it won't necessarily bring about real, physical change if it fails to shift the vibration that's actually holding them back. Don't give your power to techniques. Techniques are nothing but tools, and you have to know what the problem is before you can choose the tool that will help you fix it.

Now that you've identified how you feel, it's time to determine how you WANT to feel. If you don't want to feel unappreciated, for example, you clearly want to feel appreciated, instead. You want to feel trusted. You want to feel satisfied and successful and free to make decisions. Again, this may seem like a really simple exercise (and it is, it's all *meant* to be simple), but you'd be surprised how many people have never taken the time to figure out what it is they want instead of the stuff they spend *all day* complaining about. Remember not to get specific (remember the telescope analogy!). Don't try to visualize the actual workplace with a nice boss and awesome co-workers just yet (unless doing so feels really, really good. You can always focus on whatever feels really, really good). Instead, just sit with the feelings you want to feel for a few minutes. Do this even if you've already decided that you think you know what you want.

It's not about the stuff

You see, what you want, what you TRULY want is never going to be STUFF, or a situation. It's always going to be a feeling, the feeling that you think this stuff or situation is going to bring you. You don't really want a better job; you want to feel empowered, free, successful, appreciated, validated and proud of yourself. You don't want a hot, amazing romantic partner; you want to feel loved, in love, appreciated, validated, secure, safe, excited, sexy and passionate. You don't want a million dollars; you want to feel secure, safe, free and empowered.

When you understand that everything is just a representation of vibration, you can begin to wrap your head around the fact that what you've always thought of as the WHAT in 'what you want' is actually the HOW, as in 'how what I want will come about'. You want to feel free, and you think that the only way for you to feel free is to win the lottery.

The car or house you want is a HOW, because what you truly want is what you think that car or house will bring you. The qualities you want to see in others belong in the HOW category; you want your boss to be nicer to you because of the way you think it will make you feel. This is one of the hardest elements of this work for people to understand and accept. It often feels to them like I'm trying to get them to give up on their desires. The mind often associates the HOW with the WHAT so strongly that when you try to take one away, it feels like you're pushing both out the door. When I tell someone to stop focusing on THE ONE (romantic partner) they hear, 'You will never be loved. Just accept it already', which isn't at all what I'm saying.

In the hoodlum analogy (*see page 121*) you were following the directions to a party and ended up in the wrong neighbourhood. If the party you wanted to go to was 'love', someone might've told you that you had to find THE ONE in order to experience it. And yet, as you saw in our example, following those directions didn't get you to where you wanted to go. In fact, you ended up in a painful place. When you insist that what you want HAS TO come in a certain way, you're making the directions more important than the destination; you're insisting stubbornly that this is the way, and you will not even consider that you may be heading down the wrong path, even when the evidence would suggest otherwise (the neighbourhood becomes worse and worse). If you're stuck in an unwanted situation, if you want something that you can't seem to manifest, it's almost always at least in part because you're focusing on the HOW instead of the WHAT.

Letting go of the HOW is NOT the same as letting go of the WHAT. You get to have what you want, and it will manifest in the most awesome way possible (often way better than what you've been insisting on). What you cannot do is insist that you know what the best possible representation of that feeling is. You see your mind isn't built to figure out the HOW. It doesn't know where all the great jobs and hot men and women are. It doesn't have the power to inspire all the relevant parties to be in just the right place at just the right time. The human mind simply doesn't have the capacity to figure out what the path of least resistance, the path that will actually get you what you want, is. The good news is that it doesn't have to. This is not the mind's job. Figuring out the HOW is the Universe's job. That computer is WAY more powerful than our brains, contains WAY more information than we can and can calculate WAY more data. Our job is simply to set the course for what we want and then follow the feedback we get. That's it.

And yet, people still insist that they will never be happy if they don't meet THE ONE dude or dudette, find the perfect job, win the lottery, get that promotion at work, or lose that weight. When you do this, however, it's a bit like a child who's asked his mother for chocolate pointing to a box labelled 'Brussels sprouts' at the grocery store and insisting that this is what he wants. His mother tries to explain to him that Brussels sprouts do not taste like chocolate and that they would be better off going to the chocolate aisle, but the boy, absolutely determined to get what he thinks he wants instead of what he actually wants, throws himself on the floor and has a tantrum. If his mother then gives in and buys him the Brussels sprouts, he will, of course, complain about how this is NOT what he wanted.

What you want is a feeling, an emotion. When you focus on that emotion, thoughts and mental images will come into your mind to represent that feeling. DO NOT get locked into insisting that this representation is what you truly want, just because it feels so good to think about it. Focus on it and let it morph and change as your vibration becomes more and more clear, more and more finely tuned to what you want.

In our example with the sucky job, you can use the statements of what you don't want to help you figure out how you actually feel. Sit with each negative statement, make space and just allow the feedback to present itself. You'll begin to feel something, or even have some thoughts and memories (*see stage 3 of the Progression of a Manifestation, page 49*), manifest that you can then focus on to amplify that feeling. Once you've acknowledged how you feel, you can then use that information to figure out how you want to feel. When you hit on the feeling you want, you will already experience a shift. You may feel a physical sensation, like a tingling in your stomach or goose bumps, or you may even cry. In some cases, simply focusing on what you want is actually enough to shift the resistance to it.

Once you do figure out what you want, you can then begin to focus on that feeling and let the Progression take you through the stages. Just remember, ALWAYS REMEMBER, that what you really want is the underlying emotion. Stuff is nice, and you'll have plenty of it when you become a match to the frequency of what you want (and it will be better than you imagined!), but as long as you insist on the stuff over the feeling, you're actually trying to create a feeling by first creating a physical manifestation. Now that you understand how the Progression of a Manifestation works, you can see why that will never work.

Chapter 10

Using the Progression to Release Resistance

The key to manifesting or *receiving* everything you've ever wanted truly lies in your ability to let go of any beliefs, or automated decisions, currently blocking or negating that goal. Sometimes, simply figuring out what you truly want will already be enough to shift those limiting beliefs. This will be the case when you can already reach the vibration of what you want, meaning you're not too far from the feeling of what you want on the Spectrum. If you want to love and be loved, and you can truly generate that feeling within yourself, simply marinating in this feeling will be enough to activate the frequency of what you want, starting the Progression of a Manifestation that will match that wanted vibration. Thoughts, memories and ideas, synchronicities and experiences that feel like love will start to show up in your reality.

When there is little resistance to something you want, simply focusing on something that generates the feeling of this thing you want will be enough to make you a match to it and manifest it into your reality.

The problem arises when you can't fully generate that feeling – when you're currently in a part of the Spectrum that's too far away from the emotion you're reaching for. In that case, you'll have beliefs that are blocking you from fully achieving resonance with the frequency you want.

The fact that the Spectrum is a Progression means that you can't jump from ANGER to JOY, or from DEPRESSION to HOPE. You can *progress* there, but you can't jump. Keep in mind that incremental change doesn't have to be slow. You can progress quickly, but you do have to allow it to be a Progression, which is incremental by nature. Even when someone makes what we call a 'quantum leap', which is when you make an extreme vibrational change in your life (you seemingly jump from one part of the Spectrum to a much higher part of it), they are still going through a rather large Progression. They're just doing it very, very quickly. Even though I've made such quantum leaps, I don't recommend them for this reason: releasing that much resistance at such a high speed is usually incredibly uncomfortable. If, however, you don't care about the discomfort and still want to know how to orchestrate such a leap, I've included some resources to guide your hard-core behind in the right direction at the back of this book (*see Appendix II, page 231*).

The important point to remember is that change always happens *incrementally*. Techniques that don't respect this fact, and attempt to move you from one part of the Spectrum to any part that isn't right next to where you are *in one go*, will fail. This is why, when you actually hate yourself, you can't just chant 'I love myself! I love myself!' and have it do anything but annoy you. You cannot generate a feeling of love off the back of a feeling of hate. The two are way too far apart. You can, however, progress up through the groups of the Spectrum in order to reach love.

In the analogy with the telescope (*see page 92*), I explained why you can't focus specifically on what you don't want and then instantly shift to focusing specifically on what you do want without first backing off. You've now learnt that you back off by focusing on the emotional essence of what you want, instead of trying to define it. You find the frequency of what you want and then let the Progression bring you more and more details that match this vibration. When you have resistance, however, your focus won't be 'clean'. You'll be focusing on the frequency of what you want (or at least in that direction), but also focusing on something that contradicts (or resists) the frequency of what you want. This creates static, like when you're tuning in to a radio station, but haven't quite found the sweet spot. You can hear some music, but there's also a bunch of white noise. Your vibration in that moment is 'dirty' (and not the good kind of dirty). When you first start to focus on what you want, you will never be able to focus on it in a totally 'clean' way. You'll never be able to hit the frequency on the head exactly. The best you can do is to get into the vicinity of it and point your telescope in the general direction (at the part of town that contains the building you're looking for). You will always have static at first.

I really can't stress this enough. So many people write to me and complain that they don't really know what they want, or can't really envision what that might look, never mind feel, like. They often beat themselves up for not being visionary enough, or feel like they can't succeed at manifesting what they want because, after all, if you can't tell the Universe precisely what you want, how can you ever get it? But here's the thing: you don't have to tell the Universe what you want, the Universe already knows. Every experience you've ever had spawned desires, and this information is being held in your own, personal database. Not a single detail was ever lost. As long as you become a match to the feeling you want to achieve, and therefore a match to the frequency of what you want, the representation of this precise frequency, the stuff or experience that will feel exactly that way *to you,* will have to manifest.

Remember that your thoughts, memories and ideas, including mental images of what you want, are a result of your vibration. This means that if you are currently a long way away from the emotion you want to achieve on the Spectrum, you CANNOT envision the perfect representation of what you want. It's not a match to where you are right now. But that's totally OK. As long as you find the best-feeling representation of what you want that you have access to *right now*, you will start a Progression of a Manifestation that moves you in the right direction.

> **By continuing to focus on what you want to the best of your ability (listen for the music amid the static), you'll continue to activate the frequency of what you want, and you'll also be activating the frequency of whatever resistance is blocking it.**

Let me just take a moment to point out the significance of that statement. You have millions of beliefs (possibly more). All of them are destined to become obsolete or limiting, at some point. There's no telling how many of them are outdated at this moment. Instead of hunting through all of those beliefs randomly in the hopes of finding and releasing one that will actually make a difference in your life right now (telling your life story and hoping that something jumps out at you or your therapist as a red flag, for example), which can take *years*, you use the concepts of focus and the Progression of a Manifestation to activate the precise belief system that is currently blocking what you want. No hunting required. How exciting is that?

So, not only will you be starting a new 'positive' Progression of a Manifestation, which matches what you want – therefore making it easier to hear the music – you'll also be starting a 'negative' Progression of Resistance, which matches your limiting belief and what you don't want, so making the static more obvious, as well.

In this way, you'll be turning up the volume on both the bit of music you want to hear as well as the static. In other words, you will begin to manifest both elements that represent what you want, as well as elements that represent what you don't want. The goal is to recognize both sets of manifestations for what they are – representations – and attune yourself more and more to the frequency of what you DO want. Of course, when you do this deliberately, you don't have to wait until both of these Progressions manifests in the physical (although, it's OK if you do). You can simply allow the unwanted or 'negative' Progression of Resistance to build just enough for you to recognize what the belief system is and then change it, effectively getting rid of the static and allowing you to hear the music more and more clearly. The 'positive' Progression of a Manifestation, what you do want, will become more and more predominant, until it's the only thing left. Your manifestations will continue to get 'cleaner', until the only thing that's left is precisely what you want, with no negatives attached.

You don't have to settle for less. You don't have to pay some kind of price. You can fully experience the frequency of what you want, and all the manifestations that match it. In other words, you can finally manifest the reality you've always wanted.

The Progression of Resistance takes *exactly* the same course as the Progression of a Manifestation (see Chapter 4 or Appendix III for a quick reminder of the step-by-step process of the five stages). The only thing is, you might not realize it. Because limiting beliefs are dependent on denial (unawareness), and that denial will have almost certainly been going on for quite some time (all or most of your life) – you won't be able to feel the feedback as acutely. The negative emotions won't be as apparent. In fact, you may not be aware of them, at all. But that's OK. Remember, if you don't notice the messenger, it will knock louder. We're going to use this Progression to become aware of the resistance that's currently blocking what you want.

As you continue to focus on what you want, building both Progressions – what you want and don't want – you could feel some negative emotion (stage 2), but as I already explained, you may not notice it. This means that the first evidence of your resistance that you'll be able to engage with will often be in stage 3 – thoughts, memories and ideas. It's interesting to discover that even though you'll be doing your best to focus on the feeling you want in a general way, the feedback you'll get will often be incredibly specific. The way in which your resistance manifests will depend on what, exactly, will best represent that energy *to you personally*.

The 'yeah... buts'

As you begin to focus on what you want and enter stage 3 of a Progression, you'll begin to think of or 'see' representations of what you want, perhaps a better job. At this point, you may be asking, 'Wait a minute! I thought you said that the job was a HOW and that I shouldn't focus on it!' Let me explain: When you START with the feeling you want, and then let the Progression bring you representations of that feeling, you can use those representations to help you strengthen and stabilize your vibration. In other words, if you start by focusing on the feeling you want and the idea of a better-feeling job pops into your mind (one that actually feels good to you), you can certainly focus on that better-feeling job as long as it continues to feel good (stay on the 'positive' Progression) and as long as you don't insist that this job has to manifest exactly as you're seeing it.

So, as you focus on that great-feeling job, you'll also manifest your resistance, which will often show up as contradictory thoughts and statements. These types of thoughts are what I like to call the 'Yeah... buts'. Whenever you activate what you want, any resistance you may have will show up in the form of justifications for why you can't have what you want (or rather, the representation of what you want, such as a new job). The great thing is that even if those statements are contradicting stage 3 of your 'positive' manifestation (the *idea* of a better job), they'll still be pointing you in the direction of your limiting beliefs (your resistance).

Here are a few examples of some 'Yeah... buts':

- 'I'd love to have a bigger house! Yeah... but I can't afford it/ the housing market is bad right now/people will think we're showing off/etc.'

- 'I want so desperately to be in love! Yeah... but I'm too ugly/too fat/too poor/in the wrong town/not good enough/ etc. to get a partner.'

- 'A holiday with the whole family sounds amazing! Yeah... but my boss will never give me the time off/we can't afford it/foreign countries are scary/the garage needs cleaning and I should do that instead/etc.'

- 'I've always wanted my own business. Yeah... but being self-employed is risky/the economy is bad/I don't know what I'm doing/it would be crazy to give up my secure job even though I hate it/my family won't approve/etc.'

Everyone has their 'Yeah... buts'. Most people consider their 'Yeah... buts' as FACTS, immovable objects on the path to what they want. There's no way around them. These 'Yeah... buts', however, are just representations of our limiting beliefs.

Here's the thing: when you engage with and validate your 'Yeah... buts' at this stage, when you accept them as TRUE, you are arguing against an idea, a concept, a thought. At no point so far have you taken any action. No one has said that you should quit your job, buy that house, or go on that holiday RIGHT NOW. These are thoughts, ideas and visions. You're simply using your imagination, and when you argue with your imagination you are, quite frankly, shitting all over what you want. In fact, this is how and why most people shut their imaginations down, as they grow older. As kids, we have no problem playing pretend. We can simply imagine something for the fun of it, we can let it be a representation of fun, without needing it specifically to come true or be 'realistic'. But as adults, we have all these reasons for *why* we can't get what we want, and it's not enough that we apply these reasons to our physical reality. We have to apply them even to the realm of make-believe!

Imagine being a kid again and you've decided that you are, in this moment, an astronaut, floating in space. Now, an adult comes along and says to you, 'You are not in space. You are in the living room. That is not a space ship; it's a couch. And you are not wearing a space suit. Those are your pyjamas.' The adult's inability to suspend reality (what is real to them) would shut the game down.

Or, let's say that the adult would try to play. So, they accept that you are an astronaut. But as you play, you decide that you will visit the sun! The adult jumps in and begins to argue that you can't visit the sun, because you'd be incinerated on contact. What a dick!

When you engage with your 'Yeah… buts', you are being that dick – you're shutting down your own imagination, the tool that allows you to connect with and therefore receive the reality you actually want. But, why would you do that? Why would you insist on holding on to the rules of a reality that you don't actually want? Well, generally speaking, it's because you've been taught to buy into the Crappy Core Beliefs from Chapter 6 (that there is only one truth, you can't get what you want, beliefs are not a choice and you have to see it to believe it). There is, however, another issue: your mind has also been trained to think that it has to take responsibility for creating the reality you want (trying to figure out the HOW).

When those 'Yeah... buts' come up, recognize them for what they are – representations of your resistance, NOT actual, immovable obstacles. Remember that you *can* get what you want and limiting beliefs can be changed. In fact, doing so is actually quite simple. When those representations of your resistance pop up, you can just pluck them out, one by one, and dissect them. You are literally giving voice to your resistance. You're giving yourself a huge clue as to what your limiting belief is.

By saying, 'I'd love to get a better job! Yeah... but, the economy is in the toilet right now,' you're saying several things:

1. You can't get what you want (Crappy Core Belief #2)

2. Your ability to manifest what you want is conditional upon something else; in this case, the economy. First the economy has to get better (something you can't control), and only THEN will you be able to get a better job. Of course, you can't control the economy, so this belief is a showstopper. And even if the economy does get better, you'll still have plenty of other excuses left for why you can't actually get what you want. You see the economy is simply a representation of your belief. It's not *actually* an obstacle. These types of conditions are an indicator that you're focusing on the HOW instead of the WHAT. In this example, you need the economy to get better so that you'll get a job, and then you'll need to get a better job in order to get what you really want – to feel free, and validated, and so on.

3. You have a 'mystery belief' (any other personal belief that you inherited or adopted during childhood but in either case is based on faulty or limited data).

Since I've already covered numbers one and two extensively, let's dig into number three...

The mystery belief

Keep in mind that wanted manifestations can, and usually do, have more than one limiting belief blocking them. This simply means that you may need to repeat the releasing process a few times.

First, remind yourself and accept that you can have what you want (reread Chapter 6 if you need to), and ONLY your vibration determines what you manifest. Even the economy is simply a mirror to your energy. This won't generally clear the belief (although it sometimes can), but it will open you up to the next step.

Next, isolate the 'Yeah... but' part of the statement – 'the economy is in the toilet', along with the implication that this is an actual obstacle to you getting what you want. In this case, we're looking at a fairly simple belief: 'I can't find a great-feeling job until and unless the economy improves.' Notice that your belief is not about the economy, but rather about how the economy affects you personally. The easiest way to release such a belief is simply to contradict it. This works well with relatively simple beliefs. In order to demonstrate how to do this, here's a recap on the Five Basic Steps to Changing Any Belief and Releasing Resistance from Chapter 6:

You can change any belief by:

1. Recognizing that your current belief is based on an incomplete set of data.

2. Opening your mind up to the idea that more data, much of which will NOT support your current perspective, exists.

3. Deciding which perspective you'd like to adopt (or just how you want that perspective to feel).

4. Looking for the evidence to support that new, wanted perspective.

5. Gathering enough of that supporting data so that you can accept this new perspective as 'truth'.

Let me restate those steps to fit our example:

1. Recognize that your belief is FALSE – you understand, at least intellectually, that your ability to find a job is not tied to the economy. Notice that at this point, you will not BELIEVE this statement completely. You don't have to, but you do have to be open to exploring it.

2. Open your mind to the idea that there are jobs out there right now, which would feel great to you, even if you have no idea where they are or how to find them.

3. Choose to believe that you can manifest a wonderful, great-feeling job.

4. Allow yourself to daydream about this wonderful-feeling job. Focus on this feeling until 'evidence' that supports it manifests (you may be positively inspired to check a job board, for example), although DO NOT take action until you're positively inspired to do so. You want to gather evidence that matches your wanted manifestation, not evidence that supports your resistance.

5. When you do find this type of evidence, and it will manifest as long as you focus on the good feeling to the best of your

ability, accept it as valid. Choose to believe it. When you've gathered enough evidence to 'prove' to yourself that a good-feeling job scenario is possible, your belief will shift.

Keep in mind that this five-step process can take anywhere from a few seconds to several weeks, depending on how open to change you are and how ingrained your resistance to it is.

Case study: The 'yeah... but' in action

In my coaching practice, the process often looks like this (after I have gotten the client to focus in a good-feeling way and the 'Yeah... buts' have popped up):

Client: 'I can't get a job because of the economy.'

Me: *'Really? So, no one out there is getting a job?'*

Client: 'Well, no. I guess some people are getting jobs.' (Recognition that the belief is false.)

Me: *'Are any of these jobs good ones?'*

Client: 'Yeah, I guess some of them are.' (Opening the mind to the idea that what the client wants exists.)

Me: *'Can you imagine yourself in a good-feeling job? Can you choose to believe that you can get a great job, even if you have no idea how that might happen?'*

Client: 'Yes. Yes, I can.' (Choosing to focus on the good-feeling job.)

Me: *'Imagine this great job. What's so great about it?'*

Client: 'Well, the boss is amazing. He listens to me. And the co-workers are all incredible. It's like a family. We do awesome work. I can see us celebrating!' (Opening up to evidence.)

Me: *'Have you ever heard of anyone that has a job that feels this way?'*

Client: 'Yes! I have! My old colleague from my old company loves his job. And my uncle works for a great company...' (Gathering evidence.)

Me: *'So, do you think you could maybe find a job like that?'*

Client: 'OMG, yes I do! I'm not yet sure how, but of course, if they can do it, so can I!' (Acceptance of the new belief.)

This is, of course, a simplified version of real events, but the basic steps are there. This type of conversation might take five to ten minutes, providing the client is open to feeling better and doesn't throw up a bunch more 'Yeah... buts' in the process. If more contradictions come up, we simply repeat the process until they're all gone.

There are a few key elements I want to point out here. First, we will already have figured out how the client really feels and how they want to feel, as well as having activated that frequency. This is, actually, what brings up the 'Yeah... buts' in the first place. Second, when the client imagines the great-feeling job, we allow the specifics of that job (the awesome boss and co-workers) to manifest naturally. You cannot just say positive-sounding stuff and expect it to work. If the words don't actually feel good, go back a step and focus on the feeling for a couple of minutes before trying again. And third, if you are a coach, you can help your client by presenting them with evidence that supports their positive belief, but only once you get to step 4 (daydreaming about the new scenario), and only once they have enough momentum going. If you do this too early, your client will only argue with you. Keep in mind that the client still has to accept this evidence as valid for them. If you are working by yourself, make sure that you don't look for evidence before you're inspired to (or you'll find the wrong kind of evidence). Once you manifest even one supporting example, stay with it and others will follow. Always use the Progression of a Manifestation (*see page 48*) by focusing on what you want to get more of and allowing the Law of Attraction to bring you more of it.

I've found this very simple process of simply contradicting 'Yeah… buts' to be incredibly effective, as long as the Progression is respected and all the steps are followed. But, while I've had great success with this technique, no tool is 100 per cent effective, 100 per cent of the time. It doesn't, for example, work well with deeply ingrained beliefs. Try it out for yourself and see what happens.

Using the tool of visualization to find your limiting beliefs

While resistance often shows up in the form of contradictory thoughts and statements in stage 3 of the Progression of a Manifestation, it can also manifest as images in your mind. When this happens, we can use visualization. Now, you've almost certainly been introduced to the concept of visualizing what you want. You've probably tried it. You've probably also failed (at least when it came to the really important stuff). I'm not here to diss anyone, but in my opinion, teachers that tell you simply to visualize what you want only to have it magically appear are missing a huge chunk of the story. It's the same when you chant affirmations with no regard for the emotions the words evoke in you. You're holding the tool responsible for doing the job, like thinking you can build a whole house with nothing but a hammer (unless you are MacGyver, in which case, respect). It's always best to determine what you want to do and then choose the tools that fit the job. Visualization is a tool. It's a really cool tool. But used incorrectly, mainly as a way to create your reality, it's pretty useless.

At this point, it should be pretty clear that visualizing something does not create it. Remember that everything you want is created the second you have the experience that spawns the desire for it. Your job is simply to allow that creation into your physical reality – the receiving. Visualizing something doesn't *cause* you to receive it, either, but it does help you to figure out *why* you're not receiving something, as well as make it possible for you to shift your vibration so that you *can* receive it. In this way, visualization goes a step beyond the 'Yeah…but' technique and can be used to shift more ingrained beliefs.

Here's what visualization actually does: When your brain translates a non-physical frequency into an image (or set of images, like a movie), that's visualization. When you imagine a scenario and you can actually 'see' it play out in your mind's eye, when you can play through the scenario like a film, that's visualization. When you visualize something, you are translating energy, specifically your energy, into something you can perceive. The really, really cool part is that as soon as you can perceive energy, you can engage with it, and I've never found a better tool for engaging with and shifting energy in a conscious way than visualization. When used correctly, that is.

You can use visualization in two ways:

1. To help you figure out where your vibration is at before it has to manifest to a larger and more obvious degree (keep it in the thoughts, ideas and memories stage and clear it there).

2. To actually shift the belief.

Let's continue with the example of you hating your job and wanting to manifest a new one. There you are, having identified what you don't like about your job, acknowledged how that truly feels and determined how you'd like to feel instead. You've focused on that wanted feeling to the best of your ability. You're not exactly sure what you're feeling, so you allow yourself to slip into stage 3.

First, allow your mind free reign – let your imagination run wild. Imagine having a new job, with a new boss and new colleagues. There's no reason to think they'll be just like your current idiot colleagues, right? Only, as you allow your imagination to create the visualization, it will represent your actual vibration, not just what you want. In other words, you'll begin to visualize the good right along with the bad. You'll 'see' your boss getting grumpy for no reason. You'll see your new co-workers slack off just as much as your current ones. You may even see them being mean to you, bullying you, making you run off to the bathroom crying. *Why in Gawd's name would you choose to visualize that?* Well, you wouldn't, not consciously anyway. What you are doing is showing yourself what's actually been stuck in your vibration, by allowing your vibration to create your visualization, but in a form that you can more easily make changes to. You can't force your co-workers to be more competent. You can't cajole your boss into being nicer. You can't pick and choose your clients by no longer answering the phone. You can't change your physical reality through physical means (at least not very much). But you can attract a *new* reality that mirrors back a different vibration.

By allowing your visualization to create itself, you are essentially creating a non-physical representation that matches your current vibration, one that you can interact with in any way you like (the rules of your current reality do not apply); in other words, one that you can easily change. This change will be effortless, of course (you're just using your imagination to create a different scenario), unless your resistance gets in the way. Always, ALWAYS try it the easy way first. You'd be surprised at how often this works, meaning no further work is necessary. Always start with the easy techniques and only get more complicated if you need to.

You've now let your imagination run wild, and the vision of your new job has turned ugly. The first thing you'll want to do is to take each aspect that you don't like (idiot co-workers, for example), and contradict them with a new visualization. Do not try to change the entire visualization at once, just work with one component at a time. Imagine awesome co-workers. Now, a lot of people fail at this point, not because they're not doing it right, but because they quit too soon. Remember that it's a Progression – you have to wait for it to build up enough for you to perceive it. In my experience, most people with busy minds quit this exercise at around 15–20 seconds. That seems like a long time and, they figure, if it hasn't worked by then it's not going to work. If, however, you're willing to give it one to two *minutes*, which can seem like an eternity (you'll want to give yourself at least as much time as it takes to microwave a burrito...), you may well find that you'll begin to feel a lot better. And it's this feeling that you're after. If you're not sure if you're feeling better (due to extreme insensitivity), you can watch for the next stage in the Progression – you'll get access to more thoughts, ideas and memories that match this new vibration. *It will become easier and more natural to visualize the scenario you want.* It will also become totally unattractive to you to see it the old way. When this happens, you'll know that you've actually just released some resistance and shifted your energy.

I know that this seems like an incredibly simple technique. And, you may be asking yourself, 'Isn't this just visualizing what I want?' Yes, it is simple (and yet incredibly effective), and no, it's not *just* visualizing unless you don't take the time first to line up with the frequency of what you want. If you simply picture a scenario that looks positive without actually shifting your perspective (and therefore how you feel), you'll simply be looking at pretty pictures in your mind. It's not the visualizing that makes all the difference; it's how you use it. This is real change and it will be reflected back to you in your physical reality.

Case study: Visualization in action

Just to give you an idea of how effective this work can be, and how quickly you can shift your physical reality, let me tell you a little story from my life. I was working in a corporate job, as head of a department. My counterparts in other countries were all much more senior, with many of them having worked for the company for over 30 years. They were all from the old school of management: dictatorial, treating their employees more like soldiers or prisoners than human beings of value. I, as you can imagine, had a very different style, one that didn't sit well with these guys and they let me know it at every possible opportunity. When we had to collaborate on a large project, they insisted that I do things their way, including treating my staff in ways that were actually illegal in that country. I refused, which didn't go down too well. They proceeded to harass me by subjecting me to daily screaming matches on the phone, ganging up on me in meetings, not providing information I needed and just being all-round jerks.

This situation went on for months. I tried every physical action I could think of. I even brought in managers much more senior than them to mediate. They were, of course, brilliantly cooperative on these calls, only to return to their old ways the second it was just them and me.

I was working 18-hour days at this point and the day came when I just didn't have the stamina to continue with this onslaught. The only choice I had left was to start recording the phone calls and reporting them to HR, which would've netted them a slap on the wrist and ended my career (this was my reality at the time). I went home one Friday night, physically and emotionally exhausted. I was done with this situation. I had to be. I just couldn't take it any more. Yep, I'd reached my breaking point.

That's when I finally opened myself up to a solution. In my desperation, I declared that there had to be a better way. There just had to. I finally remembered all my Law of Attraction books, which had been gathering dust on the shelves, and decided to try and shift this energetically. I used a combination of visualization and the 'letter to the Universe' (see Appendix II, page 235), to work my way up the Spectrum from hating these 'jerks' to the point where I could send them love, and really feel it. This process took me about two hours during which I had a huge release (see page 206), and after I was done, I went to bed. I took the weekend off for once and rested. I didn't really focus on this situation. It just wasn't a concern to me any more. Something had definitely changed.

On Monday, I went to work as usual. But that was the only 'usual' thing about it. The entire situation was as though it had never really existed. These managers who had tortured and harassed me for months were suddenly cordial and respectful; they only called me when they needed to (about once a week as compared to daily) and, when they did, it was pleasant. They weren't my best friends or anything, they didn't go out of their way to help me, but all the harassment stopped. The change was so radical I actually went to the very senior manager who'd helped me in the past to find out if he'd had a little chat with them (not that this had ever made any difference before). He assured me that he hadn't.

What's more, I've never experienced such harassment from anyone, since. The vibration that had been attracting such situations into my life had been released. I was done with it and it was done with me. I'd made the change on Friday night and by Monday I was living in a whole new reality. So, when I tell you that this shit is real, that your physical reality will change and pretty quick at that, I mean it literally.

Using your memories to release resistance

You may have noticed that both the 'Yeah... but' technique and visualization work in the stage 3 of a Progression. There's a reason for this: once you get past stage 3, you are looking at physical manifestations (even synchronicities are small physical manifestations). Trying to make a change to your vibration via your physical manifestations is like trying to get healthier by adding vitamins to your poop. You need to start earlier.

While the 'Yeah... but' technique and visualization are incredibly effective, there will be times when they don't do the job. You can work with pretty much any belief, however, no matter how ingrained, by using the following 'memory technique' in conjunction with visualization – meaning that you'll try to shift your belief by visualizing first (always do it the easy and simple way first).

Let's say that you noticed that in your visualization of the new, supposedly way better workplace, your colleagues are total idiots who make your life hell. You try to contradict that scenario by seeing yourself in a workplace with co-workers who are competent and nice, but you just can't. When you attempt to see that, it doesn't feel good at all, there's no release, and in fact, it's making you more and more uncomfortable. Good. This discomfort is feedback – it's an amplification of the emotion of this one piece of resistance. You've turned up the volume on your resistance, making it easier for you to feel it. This is the same thing that happens when a Progression reaches stage 5 and beyond. The manifestations simply get bigger and more obvious, triggering an ever-greater emotional response in you.

As you sit with this one aspect of your visualization, the idea that your co-workers can't be anything but uncooperative jerks, you are actually starting a mini-Progression, one that's much more specific to the beliefs that are keeping you from having nice colleagues. These beliefs are a little more ingrained, affect more than just this situation, and your mind won't let them go quite this easily. As I said, as you attempt to change this vibration, more discomfort will come up. This discomfort will be an emotion. Feel it (time to get your emotional hands dirty again). Don't run away from it even if it's not comfortable (it won't be). Running away from your uncomfortable emotions is what got you into this mess in the first place, so give it a full minute or two. Wait for thoughts, memories and ideas to come up. Yes, you were already in stage 3 on the larger visualization, but you've now started a new Progression for just this one aspect of the job. Keep sitting with the feeling and look for a memory, an example of something that happened that perfectly represents how this situation feels. And when I say 'look for', I mean 'notice when it comes up'. Do not try to generate a memory or go hunting for it. This process happens automatically as you continue to activate a frequency. Remember to use that process.

You may be wondering if it's a good idea to focus on something that feels bad. After all, didn't I teach you to focus on what you want? Doesn't focusing on something that triggers negative emotion bring about *more* negative manifestations? Well, yes. But here's the thing: you're already focusing on this unwanted frequency. This process is simply making you aware of it, aware of how you've already been feeling the entire time. And you're doing so in a controlled manner, keeping the manifestations confined to the thoughts, memories and ideas of stage 3. You're using the same process that brings about the negative manifestations (and you freaking know *that* works, am I right?) to clear them.

Allow a memory to come up. Don't dismiss it. It won't necessarily have anything to do with your job; in fact, it probably won't. Remember that the underlying belief probably has nothing to do with your job. The key here is to recognize that as you match this frequency, as you feel this discomfort, *anything* that manifests must also be a match. You can't actually attract anything else in that moment. This means that all the thoughts and memories that enter your mind in that moment are relevant. This is an incredibly important point because just about everyone tends to dismiss the thoughts that come up as they do this exercise. They'll think, 'Oh, that can't be it. That's got nothing to do with this situation.' The memory that surfaces may seem irrelevant, but I promise you, it's not. It can't be. You with your focus have called it forth. Once again, you're not hunting through all your memories in order to find a relevant one; you're letting the mechanism of the Law of Attraction bring the relevant ones to you.

This is not an intellectual process, where you have to judge the memory to be valid or not. Trust what comes up. Take a look at whatever information is revealed. Observe and experience it. Don't try to change it, don't try to dismiss it and don't pretend that whatever happened didn't bother you (it totally did). Don't try to use spiritual and happy shiny words to describe what happened or how you felt about it. I can't tell you how many spiritual people I've talked to who were stuck in a situation they couldn't shift, who told me stories of rude colleagues or family members only to dismiss their statements immediately with a saintly 'but that's OK. I don't mind.' It's not OK and you do mind. This is exactly how you're ignoring your emotions – you decide that something *shouldn't* bother you, and you simply decide that it doesn't, even though it clearly does. That's denial in its purest form. Stop it.

Replay the memory that just came up and assume that it's valid and relevant (it always is). Engage with it. You're gathering more information on what this emotion is all about, the belief that's causing it. You are NOT trying to find the origin of the limiting belief. If an early memory comes up, great. If the memory is from last week, that's fine too. Remember that your obsolete programs were either installed as a bundle even before you were born and in the first years of your life, or depended on one of these already installed beliefs. The 'origin' could be hundreds or even thousands of years old. There's no point in hunting that down. You're simply letting the most relevant information present itself. Ask yourself:

- What happened?

- How old were you?

- How did you feel?

As you engage with this memory, your emotions will become ever more specific. You'll get more and more information. What exactly happened that made you feel this way? What were you really pissed off about? Talk or write about it if you can; this will help to keep you focused, even if you're just talking out loud to yourself. If you have the kind of mind that likes to wander, using a focusing mechanism like talking or writing can really help.

Let's imagine that a memory from your childhood comes up, where your older brother destroyed a school assignment you'd worked hard on. Maybe a diorama (do people still make dioramas?) – you know you would've gotten an 'A', but now the whole thing is in bits on the floor. You complained to your parents, but they couldn't or wouldn't help. Keep the focus on how you felt and how you feel now as you activate the memory. DO NOT, at this point, try to excuse anyone, see it from your adult perspective, rationalize that this wasn't a big deal or otherwise shift the focus from your own emotions. Recall how you felt then, not how you *should* feel now. The memory wouldn't have come up if it didn't reflect something that's active within you NOW. You're activating the frequency of the limiting belief to a larger degree, letting it bring you more information. The information will be in the form of greater details and more clarity on exactly what you were feeling. In this case, you might be surprised to learn that you felt the whole situation was incredibly unfair. Your assignment was ruined and the 'authorities' that were supposed to take care of you (your parents) did nothing. As you realize these details, you begin to see the parallel between this older incident and the situation with your colleagues. You get irrationally upset with them when they don't cooperate, because you have a belief that others WILL destroy your good work and there's nothing you can do about it.

This realization is usually enough to release the resistance. I'm not kidding. When you figure out what it is that you're really reacting to (or a representation of what you're really reacting to), it gives you the chance to make a new decision, to come to a new conclusion. This can often happen spontaneously. In this case, you might realize that you are not a child any more, and that your co-workers are not related to you. You could see that your co-workers aren't actually messing with you – they will not just come and destroy your diorama, or your report, but that this is what you were secretly afraid of and reacting to. You realize that you have a lot more power now than you did as a child, that you can speak up for yourself, and that if your colleagues ever really did cause you some kind of harm, there would be repercussions. This realization, that the danger you were unknowingly afraid of (that they would destroy your work) is incredibly unlikely to happen, can actually bring about the release of this fear.

If you had approached this issue logically, the idea that you were afraid that your colleagues might actually derail your career would've seemed ridiculous and outlandish. This is how your mind keeps you in denial – it requires the solution to make logical sense, which it generally won't. It makes no sense to be afraid that your adult colleagues will break your report by playing basketball in the house and smashing it to bits. And yet, this is exactly the kind of belief that you'll find when you go digging. It's almost always something mundane, boring, nonsensical and seemingly harmless. It's actually quite rare to find real trauma or something really shocking and big (yes, really traumatic experiences do surface through this exercise, but you'd be surprised how many people are afraid of this vs. how many people that actually happens to). Our fears seem like huge monsters under the bed, but more often than not, when we pull them out into the light, they're these cute, harmless, cuddly little stuffed animals going 'grrrrrrr'. You'll wonder how the hell you could've ever been so afraid of *that*.

Chapter 11

Using Your Emotions to Release Resistance

Releasing resistance doesn't have to be complicated. Remember always to start with the simplest techniques first. Once you identify what you don't want, focus to the best of your ability on what you do want (make sure this is an emotional goal). This can and very well may already do the trick. If it doesn't, notice what kind of objections or 'Yeah... buts' come up, then contradict them via the method I shared with you in Chapter 10. If this doesn't work, you can go deeper by using visualization, as well as memories that you've deliberately attracted to represent your resistance to gain more information about what's actually holding you back. The idea is to start simple and then delve progressively deeper until you shift the energy. In this chapter we're going to focus on releasing the most ingrained type of resistance – the BIG stuff that everyone struggles with.

Not all beliefs will budge when they are identified; these are the really tough mothers. Don't worry because now you understand the Spectrum of Empowerment (*see page 99*), you have the tools to work your way out of any frequency and into a better-feeling one. When working in stage 3 (thoughts, memories, ideas) doesn't work, we can continue the process in stage 2 (emotions). We're simply going to pick up where the 'memory technique' from Chapter 10 (*see page 184*) left off, meaning that you've already:

1. Identified how you feel.

2. Focused and activated the feeling you want instead.

3. Used a visualization to show you where your vibration is.

4. Attempted to shift that vibration by changing your visualization.

5. Sat with the aspect that didn't want to budge and started a new Progression.

6. Manifested a related memory and figured out what it was that you were REALLY reacting to.

I know that sounds like a lot, but once you get the hang of this, that entire process can take as little as five to ten minutes.

In our example from the previous chapter (*see page 187*), your brother destroyed your school project and your parents did nothing. You felt it was unfair, to say the least. But simply identifying the correlation between this event and your current manifestation of uncooperative colleagues didn't bring relief. It didn't shift the underlying belief. It's time to bring in the big guns.

As you may recall from Chapters 7 and 8, certain beliefs and their corresponding emotions can be mapped on the Spectrum of Empowerment (*see page 111*), representing different levels of empowerment. As you move up the Spectrum, you not only feel better, you also become more and more of a match to what you want (which is what causes the better-feeling emotions). So, it stands to reason that if you had some kind of map, which helped you move up the Spectrum from one emotion to another, from one belief system to another, that would be helpful. I'm about to give you that map.

Using the map

Please remember that the emotions mapped on the Spectrum aren't set in stone. The way we use words, including the ones to describe our feelings, is a very personal thing. The best way to know if you're moving up the Spectrum is to answer the question, 'Does this feel better?' Notice that I didn't ask if it felt 'good'. When you're in the lower part of the Spectrum, the next feeling you can reach may not feel good, but it will feel *better*. It will feel like *relief*. In some cases, you may need to reduce the question to, 'Which one of these options feels *less* painful?'

It's now time to bring all the parts of the Spectrum together and learn how to move from one emotion to another, preferably in a more positive direction. I'm going to give you some specific instructions on how to move from one group to another, keeping in mind that in order to work at this level, you must have already activated the energy of your resistance. If you are insensitive to your emotions, you can use the visualization and memory techniques (*see pages 178 and 184*). If you are sensitive to your emotions and are easily able to recognize how you feel, you can set yourself up by first identifying how you feel, then activating how you want to feel, noticing any negative emotions that pop up as you do, and focus on those (feel them more acutely). Please DO NOT skip these steps. They only take a couple of minutes! This shortened process will activate only the resistance that's relevant to your manifestation; in other words, the limiting beliefs that are actively blocking what you want.

Either way you are now feeling the emotion of your resistance and, yes, this will be uncomfortable. Find the corresponding emotional group on the Spectrum and use the instructions in this chapter to move yourself incrementally to ever better-feeling groups. I suggest that you read through all the instructions at least once, and then use them as a reference guide going forward.

Moving from DEPRESSION to SHAME

Remember that being in the DEPRESSION group represents total powerlessness, the feeling of lying in the alley and simply allowing the hoodlums to beat you up, while in SHAME you bargain for your safety by appeasing others with service. Most of the time, moving from a lower emotion to a higher one will entail taking on at least some of the beliefs of the higher one (temporarily). If you're in the upper register of DEPRESSION, service to others can actually bring a great deal of relief. However, the truly depressed person (in the lower end of the DEPRESSION Spectrum) will not be capable of really acting this out. Mind you, service to others isn't an activity that's exclusively performed by those in the SHAME group. Specific activities are not associated with certain parts of the Spectrum. It is the attitude with which one performs those activities that counts (the feeling you have while you do it). So, you can help others while sad, or guilty or angry or hopeful or ecstatically happy.

If you're not *severely* depressed, it can be really beneficial to go and help a friend or do some charity work. Sit with this idea and see if it appeals to you. Helping someone else doesn't have to be done in person, although that can be more powerful. And you don't have to limit your altruistic activities to humans. In fact, spending time with animals, while beneficial for any part of the Spectrum, is MOST helpful for those who are depressed. The idea is to bring your focus outwards, but in a positive way. The belief system that causes depression depends on the idea that the world is a painful, dangerous and hostile place where bad things are guaranteed to happen. In fact, since beliefs are always black and white, all or nothing, the irrational conclusion underlying this belief is that ONLY bad things happen. Again, remember that what you logically know to be true has nothing to do with what limiting beliefs you are holding on to. So, you can rationally know that the world is not just made up of evil bastards and yet, deep down, still believe that only pain awaits you. In fact, your mind, filtering out everything that doesn't match this belief, will be very adept at justifying why the good that is clearly in the world will never touch *your* reality.

As you help others, make sure that you actually get to see the benefit you're providing (you'll want to make sure you actually see the smiling faces, or read the glowing feedback, for example). This might be uncomfortable, since someone being grateful to you will directly defy your belief. What you are doing is gathering evidence from your current reality that contradicts your belief. Instead of simply focusing on a better-feeling frequency in your mind, you're looking for evidence, no matter how small, that supports the frequency you want to activate. When you have some physical evidence to focus on, it'll make it easier for you to keep on activating that new frequency.

You may have noticed that helping others is a type of action, so I'd better explain why I'm advising that when I made such a big deal of not working in the action stage. I am not advocating taking action to change your reality (as in, trying to force others to treat you differently), but rather action designed to bring you evidence that contradicts your current beliefs. This is a valid technique, but **ONLY if,**

1. The action you're taking belongs to the next emotional group in the Spectrum; and

2. It feels at least a little bit good to you when you think about it.

Never take action that doesn't feel good, and never take action to try and change your physical reality. Take action that's positively inspired, or take action by exposing yourself to an environment or evidence that feels better (going on a beach holiday is this type of action). Keep in mind that you still have to be willing to engage with those better feelings, focus on them, and accept them as real or, just like that beach holiday, the effects will be temporary at best.

For those who are severely depressed, or for those to whom the idea of helping others doesn't appeal, trying to help others won't work. And while I realize that the advice I'm about to give may seem a bit unconventional, it does actually work, when applied correctly.

The key to moving out of any emotion is allowing yourself to feel that emotion without demonizing it.

Instead of running away from it and suppressing it, step into it. Surrender to it. Give yourself full and total permission to be depressed, to be sad or to do whatever feels best. *Indulge the emotion*. People are so incredibly afraid of doing this, because they think they'll get stuck in the emotion (i.e. 'If I allow myself to be depressed, I'll be depressed forever'). But this isn't how it works. It's the *repression* of the emotion that actually keeps us stuck. This is true for any emotion, by the way.

Since depression and the less severe forms of sadness are on the lowest part of the Spectrum, the repression of emotions has generally gone on for a long time. This means, there will be a lot of sadness that needs to come out before you can truly feel better. This can also lead those who are indulging in the sadness to freak out. They think that any technique they use should make them feel better instantly; they're looking for a quick fix. And when allowing the emotion to flow out doesn't immediately relieve *all* the pressure, they again become convinced that they'll stay there forever. This is the biggest obstacle I've found when dealing with sadness. Well, that and well-meaning friends and family who try to cheer the depressed person up, so that they (the family and friends) can feel better, since looking at a depressed individual isn't fun. This is actually a type of manipulation. You do not owe it to anyone to feel better, to go out of the house when you don't want to, to engage in activities that make you uncomfortable, or to do anything that doesn't bring relief. Do your own thing.

There's actually a lot of relief in allowing yourself simply to feel what you're feeling, even when it's sadness. It feels good to lie in bed all day and not feel guilty about it. It feels good to cry, without constantly berating yourself for it. The choice at this point is not between these activities and going out *and* living a productive, happy life. The choice is between lying in bed and hating yourself or lying in bed and being OK with it. The choice is between crying and thinking it's wrong or crying and thinking it's fine. The first choice should always be to feel your emotions fully, without judgement of any kind. Let it be OK that you're feeling what you're feeling. You can't really change it in that moment anyway (the feeling is a response, one you have to acknowledge before it will change).

> **Remember that by feeling your emotions, you're opening the door and allowing the message to be delivered. By beating yourself up for your emotions, you're just slamming that door shut.**

When someone is depressed I also generally advise that they do their best to stay away from trying to do too much intellectual work, as this can become a distraction. You do not need to understand the emotion you're feeling in order to receive its message. It can be helpful for many people to gain this understanding, but it's not necessary. If you're stuck in depression, stay away from affirmations and trying to figure out what happened in your childhood that messed you up so badly. You can let memories come up (don't push anything away), but do your best simply to experience and observe. Don't try to figure it out intellectually.

Suggestions for moving out of DEPRESSION

- Do as much purely vibrational work as possible, along with simply indulging in your feelings without judgement (the no judgement part cannot be stressed enough).

- Spend time in nature (this is true for any part of the Spectrum). Don't worry, you don't have to *do* anything; just sit outside and let it work on you. Nature has a high, steady vibration, which can influence you (if you let it) into a better -feeling state. You can meditate if you like, or just sit under a tree for an hour or so. If you'd like to learn more about meditation, I've added a description and explanation in Appendix II (*see page 232*).

- Spend time with animals (again, you don't have to do anything, if you don't want to, just sit with them).

- Get lots of sleep because your vibration naturally rises when you rest.

- Spend time alone, as other people can be a part of the problem if they judge you and are constantly trying to change or manipulate you. Be very selective about who you spend time with (only those who are supportive and accepting of you).

- Stop watching TV or anything else that's negative.

- Bombard yourself with soothing music and images.

- Do your best to tend to your own needs as much as possible; and if you're at all up for it, do reach out for professional help (but again, be selective).

Depression causes us to withdraw, and there's a good reason for this. If the world is a hostile place, it makes sense to seek the safety of solitude. This is why when we're depressed, we stop engaging. The more depressed you are, the less you'll want to subject yourself to other people. And that's OK. Give yourself permission to do what feels like relief. But notice that I also recommend that you withdraw from any negative stimulus, like TV and scary books and music that talks about how everything sucks. No, you don't have to surround yourself with rainbows and sunshine (that would just make you want to puke), but you can aim for neutral, non-negative (instead of positive) input. So, instead of reading articles about how the world is ending, read some about solutions that are being proposed, and do your best to consider at least the possibility that these solutions will be implemented. Or, better yet, look at funny cat pictures on the Internet for a while.

Moving out of the DEPRESSION group for good can take time, in fact, more time than any other shift. This doesn't mean it has to take years, but think in terms of months (even one month is often enough, but please don't put any time pressure on yourself) instead of days or a couple of weeks, if you've been stuck in severe depression for a long time. It's not always going to be easy. You've repressed a lot of emotions, which means you have a lot of messages to receive. If you're merely experiencing sadness, this shift will be much, much faster. But in either case, you'll need to feel your emotions for much longer than a couple of minutes. It's not uncommon to spend several hours a day crying, over the course of several weeks. This might sound like a nightmare, but compared to feeling that way anyway for months and years while beating yourself up, it's actually not a bad deal. Keep feeling your feelings without judgement, surrender to the process, and you WILL begin to feel better.

Just about all the tools that will move you out of the DEPRESSION group can be applied to any other group in the Spectrum (actually most of the tools in one group can be applied to the groups above it, but not usually to groups below it). It's always a good idea to:

• Deliberately limit the negative input in your life.

• Go into nature.

• Help others.

• Spend time with animals.
  And it's also always a good idea to:

• Indulge your emotions without judgement; in fact, that one's a requirement for any shift you want to make.

These kinds of activities are designed to exclude the logical mind as much as possible. The lower you are on the Spectrum, the more the mind will try to interfere, so specifically focused techniques don't tend to work here. These general tools are gentle ways to shift your vibration without triggering your resistance. They have the ability to bring about change when nothing else can.

Moving from SHAME to ANGER

We're going to be spending quite a bit of time on the shame group, since it's so prevalent in our society. Remember that this group includes guilt, unworthiness and self-blame, which are all emotions that depend on the premise that we are bad, have done bad things and it's all our fault. Most modern religions have done a great job of both perpetuating and indoctrinating this belief. So, even if you're not a person that's predominantly stuck in SHAME, you will almost certainly be dipping into this group on certain subjects from time to time.

If you're moving out of DEPRESSION into SHAME, you may not necessarily notice a huge difference – both feel pretty lousy. However, in DEPRESSION, we are focused solely on the self (a withdrawal from the outside world), while in SHAME we are focused more on others (but not in a healthy, balanced way). A person in the SHAME group will engage much more with others and will have a better sense of control (they gain control by appeasing others). The further up the SHAME Spectrum we go, the closer we get to ANGER. Remember that in SHAME, we do our best to serve others, even to our own detriment, in order to appease them and garner a sense of safety for ourselves (such as running errands for the hoodlums so they won't beat us up so much). The emotion that signals that we're about to move out of SHAME and into ANGER (the next group up) is resentment. When we become resentful, it always means we're giving more than we want to, we're helping others at a cost to ourselves (which is what we do in SHAME), and we're getting sick of it. So, the key to moving out of SHAME and into ANGER is to validate this resentment.

You are not responsible for other people's lives, never mind their happiness. In fact, did you know that you're not even able to make them happy? No one can manifest in the reality of someone else. Ever.

Let's take a look at the type of people the SHAME group/vibration will attract as a mirror. When you are in SHAME – when you are trying to appease others so that you can feel safe, when you allow others to control and manipulate you in exchange for a little security – you must manifest those who are willing to control and manipulate. In other words, you have to attract someone who gets their sense of power from controlling others, someone from the upper echelons of the SHAME or ANGER groups. These are individuals who still feel powerless (you don't need to have power over others when you feel powerful), but aren't willing to appease any more. They want to actively manipulate. The more they can get others to do something for them, especially something that the other person doesn't really want to do, the more powerful they feel. This is the 'if you really love me, you'll do this for me' syndrome. These people are often masters at inducing guilt, of making you feel like you're the most awful person in the world, if you don't do this tiny, insignificant but incredibly inconvenient (for you) thing for them. Keep in mind that these people are only one step up (if that) from the SHAME group, and they often span both groups, meaning that manipulative people often also feel guilty. They're attempting to move out of the feeling of powerlessness and being manipulated by others by becoming the manipulators instead. Don't worry, you won't have to become a douche in order to move out of SHAME. I'm simply explaining the defensive mechanisms that people attempting to move from SHAME into ANGER usually employ. There's a way to do this much more constructively.

When you cater to these manipulative individuals, you are not helping them to shift their energy upwards. What you are really doing is helping to keep them stuck. You see, manipulating others might make them temporarily feel a bit more powerful, but power that's derived from others isn't real power. Real power comes from within. Manipulation is like a painkiller, at best, and when you just keep taking a painkiller to numb the pain, you never get to the root cause and so you never heal. The only way a manipulator will stop manipulating and actually look at what's really bothering them will be if their tactics no longer work. In this way, your willingness to cater to their manipulations is only enabling them to stay in denial. This is like giving drugs to someone addicted to heroin, out of the goodness of your heart. Sure, it'll make him feel better for a day, but he'll be right back here tomorrow. Nothing will have actually changed. If you want to do good in this world, stop sacrificing yourself in order to get them to stop complaining for a few minutes (at best).

You are not being a bad person if you decide to engage in self-care.

Remember that self-care is not the same as selfishness. When you stop catering to others over your own needs, you are not abandoning them, bleeding and beaten, in the desert. You're not leaving them to die. You're simply allowing them to take care of themselves, so you can take care of yourself, as opposed to you taking care of them, while they do nothing and NO ONE takes care of you.

When you find yourself getting resentful, and you will (this process happens naturally, remember, our job is just to get out of the way), validate that feeling. Don't suppress it as something that's not virtuous. Being resentful is a good thing, because it's showing you that you're ready to step more fully into your power. You're being pulled up the Spectrum. But you have to ask yourself, are you willing to go? Are you willing to feel better? If you sit with the resentment and feel it, you'll move up into the ANGER group, which has the power to move you once and for all out of powerlessness.

Once again, expressing your feelings in words or writing can be incredibly helpful. Talk about how resentful you are; let it out somehow. The key, especially in this part of the Spectrum, is to push everything OUT. The tendency is to keep focusing inwards, back into self-blame, but this will move you down the Spectrum, back into total powerlessness. The goal is to allow the energy to flow *out* of you. Think of it like an emotional detox. If you did a physical cleanse, you'd be going to the bathroom a lot. You'd be pooping and peeing and sweating the toxins out of your body. Now, imagine that you're grossed out by poop and you decide that you're going to suppress it. It wouldn't take you long to become really uncomfortable. Your emotional poop is backed up and needs to come out. Let it.

As you give in to resentment, you're going to notice that you're sick and tired of catering to others in whatever way you've been doing so. The way out is to stop doing those things. Stop giving more than you want to, even if that means that you stop giving altogether (you will not stop doing so forever, I promise. As you do this work, you'll move towards a much healthier way of giving, which will not deplete you. But you have to be willing to go through this phase to get there). Ask yourself what it is that you want to do, and do that. This will be surprisingly difficult for many of you, given that you may never have asked yourself that question. Asking yourself what you want presupposes that what you want is important, and that you can (and should!) even honour it. People stuck firmly in SHAME won't consider this a valid perspective. What they want doesn't matter. But as you move into more empowerment, what you want will become more and more important, and this is the stage at which you start paying attention to it.

The great news is that you don't have to apply this just to big decisions. Even catering to yourself in small ways can make a huge difference. If you want a cup of special coffee instead of the instant crap, go and get it! If you want to buy yourself flowers, or walk home through the sunlit park, even though it takes a few extra minutes, play with the kids instead of doing the spring-cleaning, or read a book, do so. It's time to start honouring yourself. If your friend asks you to split a pizza, but doing so means that you don't order the pizza you really want, say no. She can take the other half home and eat it tomorrow. Or, ask her to split the pizza you want, instead. Notice how quickly she says no. When you're used to allowing others to manipulate you, they're used to getting what they want, and NOT used to giving you what you want. But keep this in mind: when someone implies (or states) that you are selfish for not doing what they want, what they are really saying is this: 'What you want is not important. You should put what I want ahead of what you want, and if you don't, you are being selfish.' Who, exactly, is really being selfish here? If your friend insists that you split the pizza she wants, that you eat something other than what you WANT to eat just so she doesn't have to have the inconvenience of taking home half a pizza, and considers the idea of her compromising in the same way for you unthinkable, then you're dealing with a manipulator.

Always remember (this is the case for any part of the Spectrum) that there are more than two options, in every case. For example, you do not need to eat the pizza she wants and she doesn't need to eat the pizza you want. You can both order what you want and take the rest home. This is a compromise that caters to what everyone wants. If someone declines this compromise, they aren't really interested in you being happy. Their actual goal is to get you to do what they want, so they can feel more powerful. If what they're asking you to do is of some detriment to you, it's actually a bit of a bonus ('If you're willing to suffer for me, I must really be important').

As you begin to validate your resentment and feel it, and as you honour yourself more and more, you may begin to experience anger. This is not always the case. Some people release huge amounts of anger, while others feel only a little bit angry. In fact, since resentment is a type of anger (a mild anger), this may be all you need. On the other hand, it's also possible that your anger will be MUCH more volatile. This is when you'll want to know how to have a *constructive* anger release.

Now, most people alive today, especially those who like to think of themselves as spiritual or self-aware, will squash their anger response. They either don't understand just how valuable these emotions are, and/or they're afraid of anger. Remember that what most of us think of when we consider anger, is actually a display of *repressed* anger. If you feel angry, you have to be willing to sit with this emotion and express it (let it out) in a constructive way. The good news is that a properly orchestrated anger release is one of the most healing things you can ever do. This will catapult you right out of powerlessness and often even deposit you on the other side of the threshold. In other words, you'll feel incredible.

When you release anger destructively, it means just that: it's *destructive*. You either hurt someone, something or yourself. None of those are part of the ultimate goal of feeling better. In fact, a destructive anger release always leads to greater powerlessness and a perpetuation of more anger. There is no relief. If, in your anger, you tell your mother you hate her, punch a hole in the wall, or worst of all, turn the anger inwards at yourself, you'll end up with feelings of guilt, unworthiness, depression and, at worst, you'll end up in jail where your powerlessness is highly amplified.

A *constructive* anger release happens in a safe environment, generally alone or possibly with a trained practitioner of some kind (look for someone who can handle anger). The object of the anger (the person you're angry at) is generally NOT present. Why not? Because the anger release isn't about THEM. It's about YOU and how you feel. This is why it's not a bad thing to blame others, as long as you're doing so constructively. When you push self-blame outwards and you blame someone else, you don't have to do it to their face. They never even have to know that you've used them as an excuse to become more empowered. They don't have to be there. This is not about what they need to hear. It's not about getting anyone to understand how you feel. This is not about forcing others to make a change so you can feel better. Do not rail against them and demand that they stop manipulating you. This is about you not allowing yourself to be manipulated any more. When you fully embrace this new, self-empowered perspective, your reality will mirror it back to you. You'll attract people who have no desire or need to try and control you.

So, yes, you can rail against them, but not to their faces. It also doesn't matter whom you're directing your anger towards, as long as it's not you. This can even be someone you love. I promise you, you are not harming them in any way. You can't put the hex on them by having angry thoughts about them. Always remember that as these emotions come up to be released, they've been there all along. You're not creating an emotion that wasn't there; you're simply allowing a toxic sludge that's been festering inside you for quite some time to come out. Better out than in, I say.

Keep in mind that you do not need to try and instigate anger. Some of my clients, in their enthusiasm to have a healing anger release, have tried to make themselves angry. This doesn't really work. The key is simply to allow the anger to happen when it comes up. If it pops up at an inopportune time (like in the middle of a business meeting), make a deal with yourself to release it at the first possible opportunity. Then, as soon as you can get away to a private spot for a few minutes, do so. Or, pretend to be writing an email and write your anger out (do not put an address in the 'To' field. You don't want to send it to someone accidentally). You can delete it when you're done. Honour your deal with yourself. The more you've let your anger out, the less volatile it'll become and the easier it will be to put on hold.

Releasing anger can happen in a variety of ways, but it's always best to express it and direct it AT someone or something. Again, the object of your anger does not have to, and actually should not, be present. Although you can pretend that they're in the room while you yell at them. This is actually incredibly satisfying. You can also write a letter to them that you'll never send, which will also help you to direct your fury outwards.

Another method is to do something physical, like take a brisk walk, stamp your feet or punch some couch cushions. Physical movement gets energy flowing, which can make quick work of an anger release. Choose whatever activity you like, it really doesn't matter as long as it works for you. I do, however, have three ironclad rules for having a constructive anger release that you should never break:

Rule #1: Release the anger alone

As I already said, it's best not to have anyone present (especially not the object of your anger) during your anger release. This is for two reasons. First, you won't shut yourself down. If you're worried about hurting someone's feelings, you're not going to allow the anger release to come to its conclusion, which means you won't actually shift much energy. Second, they won't shut you down. Very few people are able to handle someone's anger constructively. It makes them uncomfortable. Often, people will shut down your anger by getting even angrier than you. They'll bully you into submission. Or, they may guilt you into stopping. In order to have a full anger release you have to keep going until you simply don't feel angry any more. You'll feel tired and spent (or possibly euphoric, although that usually comes later), but you won't feel angry any more. This is not the same as letting off a little steam. Other people get in the way of a constructive anger release.

Rule #2: Don't censor what comes out

This is where the emotional poop metaphor comes in handy. If toxins have been festering inside you for ages they will not look or smell great as they come out. That doesn't mean you should keep them in. When you have a long overdue anger release, what comes out of you will not be pretty. You will say mean and hateful things. You might even curse like a sailor (this is highly recommended, actually, *especially* if you don't normally curse). DO NOT censor yourself. Remember, no one ever has to know. But you have to be willing to express how you truly feel, so that you can get it out of you and move on. You have to be honest. Also remember that this is not an all or nothing game. You can love someone and still hate them in the moment. Being angry with someone doesn't mean that you no longer care about them. But using the fact that you love them as an excuse not to acknowledge how you feel will keep you stuck in powerlessness. No one that truly loves you would ever ask you to do that.

Rule #3: Get angry with anyone or anything EXCEPT yourself

And finally, never, EVER get angry with yourself. You can get mad at anyone or anything, but never direct the anger inwards. This will drag you right back down to SHAME or even DEPRESSION. This is the main reason that people never move past SHAME. They feel themselves naturally move into anger, but won't allow it. They shut it down by directing the anger towards themselves, moving back into self-blame, and getting stuck in a never-ending cycle of SHAME to ANGER and back to SHAME – a cycle of doom. If you don't want to get stuck there, make sure to direct your anger *outwards*.

After an anger release, especially if you've had a volatile one (lots of crying, yelling, etc.) you'll feel immediate relief. You may feel a bit tired, as I said, but you will feel better. Over the course of the next day or two, you may experience some after-shocks. You may feel the need to cry or take a nap, or sleep more. If that comes up, honour how you feel and let the tears flow, take the nap, sleep as much as you need. Not everyone has this experience, but many do. Most people also experience a period of absolute elation sometime after an anger release, some even on the same day. This euphoria is an indicator of the new, higher vibration you've moved into. As you acclimatize to that new vibration, it won't feel quite the same (things will normalize), but you'll continue to feel better.

Will you have to have a huge anger release? This is impossible to say. You may; you may not. This will vary from person to person and from issue to issue. You may release a lot of anger on one issue and seemingly skip right over it on another (you will not skip it, you will just move through it very quickly). The point to remember is this: if anger comes up as a result of focusing on what you want, just like any other emotion, engage with it, let it flow through you and out, and be done with it. Let the emotions do their job.

Moving from ANGER to FRUSTRATION

There really aren't any specific techniques for moving from ANGER to FRUSTRATION, other than to honour your emotions and allow them. Frustration seems to be something we dip down into, not something we move up into. Let me explain. When you move out of ANGER, you generally do so in, at least, a somewhat explosive way. This means that you've unblocked a large amount of energy and have shot forward very quickly, like water rushing forth from a burst dam. I have never once had to coach anyone from ANGER into FRUSTRATION.

Moving from FRUSTRATION to HOPE

If you find yourself in FRUSTRATION, however, there are techniques that will help you to move higher. Remember that FRUSTRATION is the group just below the threshold, which means this shift is about moving from powerlessness into empowerment, from being negatively focused to being positively focused. And this is the key to moving out of FRUSTRATION. In FRUSTRATION, you believe, at least to some degree, that you can and should get what you want, you're just not yet sure that you actually *will*.

Frustration is also a sign that you're trying to take action too soon. Instead of waiting for the manifestation of action (a stage 5 manifestation), you're trying to *make something happen*. You're pushing. Frustration is a sign of impatience. Never take action in a state of frustration, if you can help it. Take the time to align your energy first.

When you're frustrated, back off. Focus on what you want and let the evidence that supports the belief you want to hold come to you. Let the thoughts and ideas and synchronicities show you that you're on your way. Soothe the idea that it might not happen, by asking 'what if it does happen?' Shifting out of FRUSTRATION is not difficult. At this point, you have very little resistance to what you want. You're about to cross the threshold, which is why frustration often feels like pressure. You can feel the other side is close, just out of reach. Remember that this is a natural progression, so if you relax and let go of any need to control how things have to come about, you'll simply be carried across.

At this point of the Spectrum, you can also begin using the simple but incredibly powerful technique that I call 'poke and run', of which you'll find a full description in Appendix II (*see page 240*).

Moving from HOPE to ENTHUSIASM

The main difference between the HOPE and ENTHUSIASM groups is positive expectation. In HOPE, you're positively focused, but you're not yet sure if you'll get what you want. In ENTHUSIASM, you're totally expecting to get what you want. The one danger in expectation is that you might tend to get too specific, which is a type of controlling behaviour and stems from a lack of trust in the positive. In other words, if you don't fully trust that you will get what you want, you might be tempted to get in there and *make* it happen. If you do fully trust it, you'll let go and *let* it happen.

Moving from ENTHUSIASM to JOY

And that's also the key for moving from ENTHUSIASM into JOY – the enhanced ability to trust fully that everything will work out for you in the best possible way. In JOY, you don't need to know exactly how things will show up; you just trust them to do so. My mantra for the last couple of years has been: 'I don't know what's about to happen, but I know it will be awesome!'

Saying this puts me in a state of general positive expectation and trust that things will just be, well, awesome. And you know what? They always are.

Putting it all together

Now that you know how to move up the Spectrum incrementally, let's apply all of this knowledge to our example of the sucky job. When we last left the story, you had accessed the memory of your brother destroying your diorama, and your parents doing nothing about it. You realized that you were actually afraid that your colleagues today would somehow damage your career, but this realization didn't bring a shift. So, you have to delve deeper.

The emotion you're feeling is fear, which is another name for severe insecurity, and can reside in either the SHAME or DEPRESSION groups. Since you're feeling some anger, you know that you're actually being pulled from the SHAME into the ANGER group, which is a really good sign. Your next step would be to express that anger, perhaps by stepping into the memory and pretending that you are the age you were then, and are able to yell at your brother and even parents in a way that you couldn't, back then. Give your anger a voice. Cuss them out. You could also do this exercise with your co-workers (pretend they are in the room with you), but it's often easier to work with the memory that presented itself. Just remember not to stop until you feel well and truly done.

After expressing and releasing your anger, you'll have a whole new vibration. If you've had a big release, take a break, possibly for a few days. When you feel inspired to, go back to the whole job situation and start over from the beginning to let the next piece of resistance come up. Rinse and repeat.

What to expect after a big release

We've talked a lot about releasing resistance, and I realize that aside from what I wrote about moving from SHAME into ANGER (*see page 200*), I haven't really described what it feels like to shift energy. The truth is that it's usually quite obvious, unless you're stuck in the numbness that comes from repressed anger. Most people, unless they are totally numb, feel some kind of physical release, like a whoosh in their stomach, a tingling, and a palpable sense of relief. Larger releases of energy will be accompanied by a 'purge', a physical release of some kind, like crying, yawning very deeply, sensations of energy running through your body and, in more severe cases, diarrhoea and vomiting (although these usually go along with quantum leaps, NOT the techniques I've presented here).

I've already mentioned the aftershocks that often happen after a large shift, such as the ones that accompany a large anger release. But it's also possible to experience physical symptoms, such as a sore throat, flu-like symptoms or aches and pains. If this happens, DO NOT panic. Understand that as manifestations progress, they become more and more physical. This means that as you hold on to resistance, which literally blocks your energy from flowing freely, it will begin to manifest physically, including within your body. When you're stressed out, for example, your body goes through damaging biomedical changes. Your emotions affect your health and often in ways you were never aware of. When you shift the blockage, the energy flows and the body can repair itself. This is when you'll experience symptoms. They are nothing to be afraid of; you're actually healing. If you know that you had an energy release yesterday and you have a runny nose today, there should be no great mystery as to where it came from. Simply see it as evidence that your physical body is now coming into resonance with your new, successfully acquired vibration.

Chapter 12

Manifesting the Reality You Want

This is the chapter you've been waiting for. It's now time to take all of the information I've presented, put it together and use it to actually manifest the reality you've always wanted. It's time to deliberately receive. First, let's review the basics of what we've covered so far:

- Everything is energy.

- You are in a holographic room, projecting your vibration to the cosmic mirror, which reflects it back to you as a physical reality.

- You can control your vibration by choosing what to focus on.

- You may be focusing on something unwanted, due to your 'search filters' or limiting beliefs making it seem like the stuff you want to focus on doesn't exist.

- Your emotions are your feedback system that let you know if you're focusing on something wanted or unwanted.

- All manifestations, good and bad, follow a Progression that is powered by the Law of Attraction.

- You can use the Progression of a Manifestation (*see page 48*) to find your limiting beliefs and release them.

- Releasing a belief is basically a matter of figuring out what erroneous conclusion you're still holding on to and changing your perspective on that subject, and you can do that by using the Five Basic Steps to Changing Any Belief and Releasing Resistance (*see page 77*).

- Your emotions are messengers who will only go away once you receive the message.

- You receive the message by engaging with or *feeling* your emotions without judgement.

- You can use this release of emotions to work your way up the Spectrum.

We've explored how the mechanism of reality works, that you are a manipulator of energy, that you have way more control over your experience than you ever thought and, even more importantly, exactly how to exercise that control. But what good is all this wonderful knowledge, if you can't apply it to actually get what you want? That's what this chapter is all about. You know how the car works; now it's time to put your keys in the ignition and actually drive it.

Manifesting something you want into your physical reality is simply a matter of becoming aware of it, of attuning yourself to the frequency that this thing you want represents to you. As you may recall from Chapter 4 (*see page 41*), you have two opportunities in the manifesting process either to attune your vibration to what you want or mess it up – the selecting and ordering of what you want from the Universe's online store (the sending out of your vibration, or what you're focusing on), and the receiving of it (how you choose to react to your manifestations). You already know how to focus on what you truly want; you find the essence or frequency of it, the emotion that it represents to you, and focus on that to the best of your ability, fine-tuning as you go. This fine-tuning is made possible by your understanding of and attention to your feedback mechanism – your emotions, then thoughts, memories, synchronicities and finally physical manifestations and action. We've spent the majority of this book dissecting your emotions and what they mean, as well as learning how to use the Progression of a Manifestation to engage with the 'thoughts, memories and ideas' stage, and find and release your limiting beliefs. You learnt that while you can't really force other people or situations to change with action, you can manipulate your reality in the energetic state, causing real changes in your physical reality. When you make changes to your vibration by controlling your focus, your reality quickly begins to follow suit.

If you remember the stages of the Progression of a Manifestation (*see page 48*), you'll recall that how you react to the feedback you receive actually sets up the next Progression. This means that your reaction is incredibly important to whether or not you're attuning yourself to what you want. The good news is that you've already laid the groundwork to changing your reactions simply by reading this book. Chapter 6, which dissected the Four Crappy Core Beliefs We All Share (*see page 75*), basically dealt with the mind-set you need to adopt in order to manifest the reality you want. This mind-set is part of what determines your reaction. If, for example, you believe that your perspective is the only 'right' one, you will never be open to changing that perspective. If you believe that you have no control over your reality and that what you see in the physical *is how it is*, you'll react to every manifestation as though it was fact, and not part of a malleable field of energy that can be shaped into anything you like. The groundwork has already been laid, but now it's time to fine-tune your ability to react in a way that's optimal to manifesting what you truly want as quickly as possible.

The concept of precursors

Always remember that what you *truly* want is always going to be a feeling of some kind. You may think that you want a better job, or a house, or a boyfriend, but what you *really* want is the feelings that you think those experiences will provide. I cannot stress this enough: what you're after is the frequency, not the stuff that represents it. This is true no matter what you've decided that you want.

This isn't to say that the stuff isn't important or fun. It's both of those. But when you focus on the representation of the frequency instead of the frequency itself, when you make the stuff more important than the feeling, you're actually starting a new Progression – one that leads to disappointment. Remember that all manifestations are part of a Progression. So, any given manifestation may or may not be a perfect representation of the frequency that you want. In fact, since they manifested as a result of your mixed vibration, **most** of them won't be **a perfect match**. You're focusing on what you want and also activating what you don't want. These manifestations are in your reality to help you fine-tune your vibration.

All manifestations serve a dual purpose: they give you something to focus on that feels *more* like what you want (or rather, what you've been focusing on, unwanted or wanted, but let's say wanted in this example), making it easier to keep on focusing that way, AND they help you to identify any resistance you have. Physical manifestations will trigger a stronger emotional response (they are more obvious representations) than non-physical ones. Unless you're already a match to something (which means you're experiencing it), your vibration on that topic will always be mixed (with some of what you want and some of what you don't want). So, most of the manifestations in your reality are going to contain both wanted and unwanted elements. If you're going to notice and work with these elements to keep making improvements on your reality, you'll have to acknowledge their significance.

If, for example, you've been working on your vibration regarding that job you want, you may wake up one Sunday morning with the urge to check the paper (inspired action), and see an ad for the perfect job. If you now decide that this job is obviously THE ONE, you may actually be focusing on something that doesn't quite match what you want, but will match only *some* of what you want. Your vibration, at this point, may not be completely 'clean' yet. But, by focusing on this manifestation as though it was the Holy Grail of jobs, you begin a new Progression – one that *may* get you that job (or something that feels like it). Also, it may not. Either way, you won't be happy.

You see, you don't know everything there is to know about that job. That's always the case, no matter what kind of manifestation you're talking about (job, person, house, car, etc.). You only see what you're able to, what is currently a match to your vibration. If you shift your vibration, you'll begin to see and experience something else. When you saw the job description in the paper, it sounded perfect. It was a synchronicity that felt good and therefore showed you that you were on the right track. But, what you don't see is that the job also contains a whole lot of 'other' elements, stuff that's not on the list of what you want. The boss is actually very nice, but he's about to leave for another department and his replacement is a real douchebag. The job description may sound great, but there are a lot of other duties that aren't listed, which will drive you up the wall. You can't know any of these things without taking the job. You can't know that this job only *seems* to have the elements you want, enough to match your vibration as a synchronicity or minor manifestation, but also contains a whole lot of other stuff, which you really, really don't want.

The good news is that you don't need to know any of that stuff. As long as you recognize this job as a synchronicity and don't hold it responsible for being the ultimate manifestation you're looking for (the ONE), you'll continue to manifest bigger and bigger versions of what you want until your dream job appears. If, however, you decide that this job is the ONE you've been looking for, and you apply for it, interview for it and do everything in your power to get it, one of two things will happen. Either, you'll get the job, find out it actually sucks worse than a vacuum cleaner on steroids, and be disappointed. Or, you'll not get the job (as a result of not being a match to a sucky job, thanks to all the positive focusing you did), see THAT as a failure, and be disappointed. No matter what, you're disappointed. Neither way gave you what you wanted and, of course, neither was ever supposed to.

These manifestations that seem to match what you want, but don't, are what I call *precursors*.

- A guy that seems to be everything you want but is unavailable to you is a precursor.

- A house that seems totally perfect but has a price you're not comfortable with is a precursor.

- A job that matches your whole list of what you want but is in a location you don't want to move to is a precursor.

> **Precursors are synchronistic manifestations that are a match to what we want and what we don't want, although we may initially only see them as positives. They can serve as signposts, letting us know that we're on the right track.**

Precursors are not meant to be your final manifestation. They are not what you want; they only seem like what you want. You are not meant to engage with them fully, only to use them as focusing tools.

How can you tell a precursor from the real thing? Well, for one, it doesn't come fully into your reality, or at least not easily. In other words, there's something about it that doesn't feel good. That guy who won't ask you out isn't a sign from the Universe that you're supposed to stalk him. Precursors also often have one glaring thing that's 'wrong' with them. A price that's too high. A perfect guy who's married. A great job in a horrible location. Or they're just a pain in the ass in some way. Essentially, any manifestation that doesn't completely match what you want is a precursor.

Unfortunately, most people in our society are so conditioned to manifest what they don't want, that when stuff that feels good actually starts to enter their reality, they freak out and begin to latch on to the first good thing to show up in years. They don't yet trust that things can get even better, but instead are incredibly willing to *settle* for something less than what they truly want. It's this willingness to settle, and the belief that we have to, that mess up more manifestations than you might comfortably want to imagine.

Manifestations that match what you want will come into your reality so easily, so smoothly, so effortlessly, they'll feel like they were always there, you only just noticed them now (and that's pretty much exactly what happens...). You NEVER have to settle for less than that. Of course, you can if you want to, but you don't have to. You can ALWAYS get what you want. But you can't have it both ways. As long as you're willing to settle for less than you want, you won't be a match to what you do want, and won't be able to receive it.

Catalogue shopping

Instead of instantly latching on to anything and everything that feels remotely good, as soon as it enters your reality, and declaring it to be the ONE, I'd advise using a technique I call 'catalogue shopping' instead. Catalogue shopping is pretty much exactly what it sounds like.

When you're looking through a catalogue, and you see a shirt you like, you never assume that you have to order everything else the model on that page is wearing. You understand that you can order the shirt from page 256, the shoes on page 125, the scarf on page 77, and the trousers from page 249. In other words, you choose the items or components that you like, and you leave the rest.

When you're looking at your reality and what's manifesting in it, engage in catalogue shopping. For example, let's say you interview for a job that seems perfect, but which would require you to move to Alaska. As beautiful as you find Alaska, you don't want to live there. Now, instead of lamenting that you're missing out on your perfect job, or forcing yourself to move to a place you don't actually like, take the components that this job had which matched what you wanted (the job itself, the way the co-workers got along, the competent, cool boss, etc.), and leave the stuff you didn't like (the location). Focus on the stuff that feels good to you and ignore the stuff that doesn't. Recognize that this job was simply a precursor, and continue to become a match to the frequency of what you want. This is how you manifest the reality of what you want.

This seems like such an easy and simple point, but believe me, it's one of the most difficult concepts to grasp when it comes to real life. I can't tell you how many clients I've argued with, because they insisted that a certain love interest was the ONE, even when it was blatantly obvious that they were not. The reason we hang on to our precursors so vehemently, the reason we're so willing to settle for something less than what we want, is in large part due to the underlying Crappy Core Belief #2 – that we can't get what we want – and any smaller supporting beliefs that formed on top of it. When you KNOW that you can get what you want, you don't generally settle. If you already have a kick-ass job offer on the table, you're not going to settle for a crappy little job that only somewhat matches what you want. When you're deeply in love with your soul mate, you're not going to settle for someone who merely 'treats you nice… most of the time'.

The only reason to settle is fear. When you're afraid that you will not get what you want, you'll grab on to anything that comes close. You'll make do. And you might even be satisfied, for a while. Until you realize that this manifestation, this man, this woman, this job, this house, this car, isn't actually what you want (basically, when you come out of denial). That's when the whole process starts all over again. You realize that you're not happy, you identify what you don't want, focus on what you want instead, begin the Progression of a wanted manifestation and then… probably latch on to the first good thing to come into your reality. While this 'good' thing may be slightly better than the last thing you gave up, allowing you to grow and evolve in this way, I'd like to point out that this method of growth is slow and rather frustrating. And that's providing you wait until something is enough of a match to you so that it can actually manifest fully into your reality. If you latch on to something too early, you won't even manifest the precursor (you don't even get an interview for the perfect-seeming but imperfect job), and you'll feel like a total loser.

It really is so much easier, faster and more enjoyable to continuously focus in a way that feels good and allows your manifestations simply to unfold. See your entire life as a giant catalogue, because it is. Every detail you see is something you can choose or something you can dismiss. None of it is 'fact' or 'how it is'; it's all something that could be. It's all just possibility. Sure, you may have manifested a job with a bunch of douchebag idiots, but that doesn't mean that you have to choose to manifest that tomorrow, or the next day, or the next.

It's up to you, though. You can do it the painful way, if you really want to. After all, it's your reality.

Beyond the threshold

I've spent the majority of this book on the lower part of the Spectrum, below the threshold, and there's a good reason for that. You can't consistently hang out in the upper part of the Spectrum without having focused (knowingly or unknowingly) on what you want MORE of the time than what you don't want. You'll have to already have released a lot of your most limiting beliefs. And, you'll have received a lot of clarity in various forms (remember that as you climb up the mountain, you get a better view). You know from looking at the emotions and beliefs in the Spectrum that continuing to move upwards simply requires that you commit yourself to focusing on what feels better, and fostering more and more trust in the idea that life is actually a wonderful adventure that's always working out for you.

But what if you're already a pretty Happy Shiny Puppy? Is there a way to speed up your progress, smooth out the ride and go further down the rabbit hole? Well yes, of course there is. Here are the most important points to remember:

- All emotions are valuable. DO NOT demonize your negative emotions. DO NOT see them as a sign that something has gone wrong. Nothing ever has. Negative emotions and manifestations appear in order to help you release the underlying limiting belief. They are helpful messengers. So, if you really want to turbo-charge your manifesting ability, see every negative manifestation as a good thing. Celebrate it. Approach it with an attitude of 'Oh yay! Something to release! And once I've released it, I'll go even further!'

- All manifestations are precursors to a degree. Because your 'goals' will always be evolving, because you're always creating new desires, no representation of a frequency can ever permanently match every vibration you may want to attune yourself to. Detach from the idea of holding on to stuff, focus on the essence of what you want, and allow the manifestations to morph continuously to mirror that back to you. This is called practising detachment. You don't need to detach from what you want, just from the representations of it (the stuff). This is much easier to do when you understand that they are, in fact, just representations.

- When you become frustrated, back off. When you're hanging out mostly in the upper half of the Spectrum, FRUSTRATION will often be the lowest you'll dip. Remember that frustration is a sign that you're pushing, that you're trying to make something happen, that you're taking action too soon. Back off and relax. Focus on the essence of what you want and get back on the Progression that feels good.

- Remember that you cannot focus specifically on a problem and immediately become a match to the specific solution. You have to back off, take a broader view and then let the Law of Attraction narrow your focus. If you're trying to figure out something with logic and you're getting frustrated, see Point 3.

- Remember that nothing is happening TO you. It's all happening FOR you. This is your game. You are in control, just not in the way you thought you were. It's your reality and you do get to have what you want.

This is truly the best time to be alive. The vibration of the entire Universe has never been as high as it is now. More and more people are waking up, crossing the threshold and becoming conscious of who they really are. More and more people are letting go of the Old World thinking, the limitation, the jealousy and hatred and anger, and allowing themselves to believe that there has to be a better way. More and more people are reaching their breaking points, are standing up and fighting back, are giving voice to their feelings, finally starting their journeys up the Spectrum. You chose to come here NOW for this reason. You are not here by mistake. Everything you are and everything you've experienced so far has been orchestrated perfectly. You came into the fog because you knew that you could find your way out, and you knew it would be the height of awesomeness to do so. You didn't come to suffer. You didn't come to prove yourself worthy. You started playing this game because you wanted a challenge worthy of a master, such as you are. You didn't want to be bored. You didn't want it easy. But you did want to win, and you knew that you could.

Conclusion

Bottom Line

You've just been given the code for the game. You've just been given the rules, hidden trap doors and all. You've peeked under the hood; you know how it works. The question remains, now that you hold the knowledge of how the Universe works, what will you choose to do with it? Will you manifest the reality you want? Or will you continue to follow the directions that someone else gave you, running into neighbourhoods you don't want to be in, and getting hurt? Will you choose to become conscious?

Will you choose to be who you really are?

My suggestion is, of course, that you give it a try. Simply *choose* to believe that this is how it actually works and use the techniques in this book to change the way you feel. You don't necessarily have to tell anyone that you're doing this, if you don't want to, but inside your own mind, be *willing* to give it your all. Don't half-ass this, instead take the following five actions:

1. Really pay attention to how you feel, and then receive the messages from your emotions by feeling them without judgement.

2. Focus on what you want, rather than on what you don't.

3. Use your tool of imagination to reach for what you want.

4. Then the tool of faith to believe that it can and will come about.

5. Use the tool of willpower to shift your focus from something that feels bad to something that feels *better*, and move up the Spectrum.

Do this for a short while (even a week will yield results) and see what happens. You'll be amazed at how quickly your reality begins to change when your focus is on how you feel. You'll gape in shock and awe at how easy it will be to change your life, even the stuff you've been struggling with for years. You'll remember just how powerful you really are, that you're a master at this, once you begin to play the game as it was always meant to be played. You'll do what you came here to do. You'll be who you always, deep down, knew you were.

I'm not asking you to take my word for it. Just try it, but try it wholeheartedly. Don't trust me. Trust the process. Trust the game. Trust yourself.

And when your life begins to change, when you become a Happy Shiny Puppy, when you begin to feel better than you ever thought you could, when you free yourself from the shackles of your limiting beliefs and you begin to annoy those around you with your new-found giddiness, come on over to my blog and join the community (the Happy Shiny Puppy Army! Please see the Appendix for additional tools and resources). I cannot wait to hear your story!

Until then, allow me to send you smooshy Happy Shiny Puppy hugs.

With all my love, appreciation and light,

melody Fletcher

Appendix 2

Bonus: How We Can Influence Other People

Ready for more?

I'm so happy that you've manifested this book! And I can't even tell you how appreciative I am that you've decided to read it all the way through!

As a special thank you, I'd like to offer you a bonus chapter, on 'How We Influence Other People'. Although this subject could easily qualify for a book on its own, I decided to try and squeeze it into a big old chapter. Unfortunately, the book was getting too long and we had to cut it, but through the use of modern technology, you can go and read that chapter online RIGHT NOW!

I've set up a special page on my website, just for the readers of this book: www.deliberatereceiving.com/additional-resources-dr-book

While you're there, you can also join the steadily growing Happy Shiny Puppy Army, an online community of like-minded individuals (other people just like you!) who support each other in the goal to make the world a happier, shinier place one puppy at a time.

Go on. You know you want to.

And, you're welcome.

Appendix II

Universal Tools

You may be wondering why I left the tools until the appendix, almost like an afterthought. After all, isn't this the *good stuff*? Isn't this what most people want – to be told exactly what to do in order to manifest something they want, like a car or a lottery win? Well, yes, it's what most people think they want, and it's what most other books on the subject of manifesting and the Law of Attraction focus on. The problem is that if that information were enough, you wouldn't have ever picked up this book! Understanding how the underlying mechanics work, and therefore what those various techniques actually do, allows you to apply any technique that resonates with you, know what to do when it doesn't work, and make the necessary adjustments in order to ensure your success. In other words, it's the difference between being shown how to use a hammer and being shown how to build a house. Once you know how to build the house, you could use a hammer or a rock or all kinds of other 'tools' to do the job. You could become like freaking MacGyver. If all you know how to do is use a hammer, you can drive a nail into a board. Yeah... that sounds exciting.

So, yes, I've left the tools for last. *You're totally welcome.*

Coming up are some Universal tools, meaning, tools that can be used in multiple if not all of the stages of the Spectrum.

★ *Meditation* ★

Yeah, yeah, yeah, I know you've heard about meditation before. *Everyone* talks about meditation. But before you skip this bit, thinking that you've been there and done that, hear me out. After all, do you actually know what meditation does? Do you know why it works or, in many cases, doesn't work?

Meditation, as most people understand it, is the process of clearing the mind of all thought. Now, if you've ever tried to do that, if you've ever just tried to shut your mind up and found it hard, you might have concluded that you just can't do that, and you know what? You were right. You truly can't just get your mind to stop thinking. And here's the dirty little secret: no one can. Now that you understand that thoughts are manifestations of vibration, it will make sense that you can't just stop a Progression of a Manifestation (at the thought stage or any other) by deciding to shut it down. In fact, the more you try to do that, the more you'll focus on what it is you want to stop; and the more you focus on that, the further down the Progression you'll go. That's right. You'll get even more thoughts. In fact, your mind will go crazy with thoughts.

What a successful meditation actually does is bring you to neutral (Zero Point on the Spectrum). You focus in a way that brings no response whatsoever, and starts no Progressions, either positive or negative. This is why focusing on a nonsensical or neutral object, sound or idea can bring us into the meditative state. If you focus on something meaningless, you will have no reaction to it and will, in that moment, stop all (or most) Progressions. At least this is what traditional meditation is all about. The purpose of this point of neutrality is that it causes you to stop your negative Progressions, even if you're not aware of them. When you then return to the 'real' world, when you reactivate all of your Progressions, you're much more likely to feel the discomfort of all your active resistance. In other words, the stuff that you were in denial about will become more obvious. Meditation is a great tool for helping you to break out of denial.

You can use any number of techniques to achieve this meditative state, but here are a few of my favourites, especially designed for people with busy minds:

- Breathe deeply and count your breaths. Each breath in and out counts as one. You may need to get to 100 before you reach a state of peace (you will feel the relief of the non-negative state).

- Do a physical activity that requires almost no attention and which allows your mind to wander, like washing the dishes, running on a treadmill, knitting, sanding something, gardening, or just walking. It's best to choose something repetitive and mind-numbing. Do you see where I'm going with this? Basically, you're going to let it numb your mind, but consciously. If you allow yourself to be aware of the numbness, of the emptiness, of the thoughtlessness, you will be in the meditative state.

- Listen to instrumental music. Again, make sure it's not your favourite song from your honeymoon. The music should not be associated with any specific memories. And you may not want to choose music with singers, if you tend to pay attention to the lyrics. I find classical music works well for me. Just lie back and let the music work on you.

- Go sit in nature. Seriously, just go sit under a tree or in a garden. Now, engage your senses — listen to the birds singing and the leaves rustling, smell the grass and the flowers, feel the sun on your skin, the breeze on your face, etc. This is, incidentally, one of the easiest ways to get into the meditative state since nature's high vibration will support you. If you have access to nature at all, use it.

- Play with a dog, cat, or other pet, or a baby. As you focus on your pet or the baby, you tend to let go of all the stuff that's bothering you and become present in the NOW. When you're present in the NOW in a totally allowing way (you're just letting the moment be what it is, without trying to change it), you're in the meditative state.

You'll know that you're doing it right when you feel a sense of profound relaxation wash over you. That will happen when you stop the negative Progressions of Resistance you've got going.

As you may have noticed, there's no mention of sitting in the lotus position while chanting 'Om'. You can certainly do that if you want to, and if you're that bendy, but I've found that particularly Westerners don't generally respond that well to this type of meditation. You see we depend on our mind all day. We're not sitting on some mountaintop in the Himalayas, Om-ing away. We've grown up thinking that our mind has all the answers. We have jobs and kids and cars to drive and groceries to buy and our mind helps us with all of that. We can't really just shut them off or tell them to get out of the way. But we can work with them. This is what all of my explanations are about. When your mind understands the process, what you're doing and why you're doing it, when it understands how it works, it will often get out of the way and let you go about your business. When we give our mind a job as we meditate, as these techniques do, we tend to have a lot more success.

You can take your meditations to the next level by making them 'active'. An active meditation is one that uses the neutral, non-negative state as an opportunity to activate a positive frequency. You see, when you stop the resistance, you'll be removing the blockages to what you want, allowing you to become more of a match to that. Use any technique you like to get into the relaxed, neutral meditative state. Then, from that place of neutrality, begin to focus very generally on what you want (the essence or feeling of it). You'll notice that the positive Progression will not only build much faster than normal, but it will also go further than you've gone before. You'll get visions that are much bigger than anything you may have achieved before. You may even see yourself changing the world! Keep in mind that whatever you're seeing is not a premonition of the future, but a representation of the frequency you're lining up with. Your actual manifestations may or may not come about in that way.

Meditation is a tool that can be used in any part of the Spectrum.

✸ ✸ ✸ ✸

✷ Letter to the Universe ✷

This is probably the most popular technique I've ever taught. You can use the letter in any of the groups in the lower Spectrum and all the way up to HOPE. Any higher than that and it tends to focus us a little too much on the unwanted to be helpful. It's also a great tool to use when you're feeling stuck or desperate, or when you need something to happen quickly and you have no idea how that might come about. It's simple, it takes about 20 minutes and it works, often incredibly quickly. I've used it with great success in my own life many times, including to shift the situation with those mean managers I mentioned in Chapter 10 (*see page 182*).

For example, a few years ago, I had made a commitment to a friend. I keep my commitments; it's important to me. However, a new and much better opportunity came up and, well, I really wanted to take advantage of it. I didn't want to let down my friend, but I also didn't want to miss out on this wonderful chance. I was really conflicted about it and had no idea what to do, so I wrote a letter to the Universe. What I really wanted was to take advantage of the new opportunity, but for my friend not only NOT to be mad at me, but to understand completely. I wanted to have my cake and eat it. I wrote the letter at night. The next day, I sat down with my friend and explained the situation. Even though I'd been so stressed about telling her, I found the perfect words and she heard me completely. She wasn't angry. She was happy for me. She completely understood and told me that in my position, she'd do the same.

This may seem like something small (it was actually a rather large commitment), but avoiding a major argument with someone I care deeply about is pretty important to me. After that, I started to use the Letter every time I found myself really stressed about anything imminent. I had no time to figure things out. A volatile business meeting the next day, an apartment search for which I had very little time, an interview for a major job promotion, etc. And each time, the Letter allowed me to release my resistance, line up with what I wanted and get the results that I was after. Ready to hear how to use it? Here we go:

Step 1: Dear Universe...

Sit down and begin writing a letter. You can just open a text file on your computer or you can make a little ritual out of it by using beautiful stationery and a special pen. It's up to you. Do whatever feels right. Date the letter and begin with 'Dear Universe'.

Step 2: Describe where you are right now

Tell the Universe about your current situation; essentially describe the problem. Be honest about how you feel.

For example: 'Dear Universe, I have one month to find a new apartment and I feel totally stressed out about it. The landlord came by today and told me that I have to move. There's nothing I can do.'

Step 3: State your fears

List all the reasons that you're stressed out. What are you afraid of? What do you NOT want to have happen? By doing this you are acknowledging the negative emotion that's already there, and allowing yourself to identify it by using the Progression of a Manifestation to release resistance (*see page 165*).

For example: 'I'm afraid that I won't find a place in time. I don't want to live in some crappy, horrible room, with nasty roommates. I'm afraid I won't be able to afford anything nice or even decent. I'm afraid that I'll be homeless or I'll have to go and beg friends to stay on their couch. I'm afraid I won't even have time to look for a new place, what with work and all…'

Allow yourself to feel these fears. As you give yourself permission to acknowledge how you truly feel, you may well find that you're already releasing (you may begin to cry, for example). You may also find that you'll get angry. If this happens, go ahead and let the anger out. Keep going until you feel that you've stated all of your fears and everything you're worried about. Just getting it all out will already help.

Step 4: Tell the Universe what you want

Now that you've gotten all the fears and doubts out of your system, go ahead and tell the Universe what you want instead. What do you need? What do you want? Remember to start off with the essence of what you want. Don't get too specific too quickly. Keep writing until it feels really good. What you're doing here is focusing on the frequency of what you want and focusing on it like gangbusters. When you begin to feel better, you'll know that you're doing it right.

For example: 'I want to feel good. I want to feel secure. I want to feel like everything will work out. I want to be in my new apartment. I don't want to have to worry about how it comes (you may put a statement about what you don't want in there, but if you do, just make sure the next statement turns it around to what you want instead). I want that apartment to come to me easily. I want it to just find me. I want a place that I'll afford easily. The apartment is close to my work and has easy access to public transport. It's central and surrounded by all the shops I need. It's bright, full of natural light and the other people in the building are all really nice. I don't have to look for the apartment; it just kind of finds me. It's easy. I can't believe how easy it is. The landlord is amazing and wants me as his tenant. In fact, he only asks me for a small deposit so that it's easier for me to afford the move. Even the move itself is easy. My friends help me and then we have a little party in my new place. I can't believe how amazing my new apartment feels. It's cosy and homely and the previous tenants even left me some amazing furniture. I love it. It showed up in plenty of time and I didn't have to worry at all.'

Notice how, over time, the writing style switched from something you want to something that already exists ('the apartment IS this and that...') to something you already possess ('I can't believe how easy it was...'). As you activate the frequency of what you want more and more, it will become more and more real to you. It will begin to manifest in a more obvious way. If your writing style starts to change, LET IT. This isn't about grammar. It's about lining up your energy. Get so into your vision and keep writing about it until you can see yourself there – in your new apartment, having found it and moved into it easily. Feel the relief of it. There's nothing to worry about. You've already got it and you're looking back on how you worried and you're seeing how ridiculous it was to be so stressed out. It all came together so beautifully! Now, you're really just telling the Universe about it, because you're so excited.

Step 5: Thank the Universe for a job well done

And that brings us to the next step. Tell the Universe 'thank you' for fulfilling your wish. It's done. What you want is on its way. You don't have to worry about it. You can just sit back and expect it to happen. Tell the Universe how awesome it is, how creative, how amazing and how you're in awe about how it led you and this apartment together.

What you're doing here is this: you've worked yourself into a higher vibration, you've aligned more with what you want, and you're now stabilizing that new vibration by entering into a state of gratitude or appreciation, which are both emotions from the upper Spectrum (*see page 111*). If you had tried to appreciate the apartment before you did this exercise, from a place in the lower part of the Spectrum, you wouldn't have been able to get there. But once you've incrementally slid up the Spectrum, appreciation becomes available and can be used as a tool to further activate a frequency.

Step 6: Let it go

You can make a ritual of this by printing the letter out and signing it, even placing it in an envelope and addressing it 'To the Universe'. You can put it in a special box or burn it or throw it in the ocean (use biodegradable paper). It doesn't matter. People use all kinds of methods to help them let things go. And that's what you're going to do now: let it go. You've 'sent' this desire and all the associated fears and stress off to the Universe. Trust that you've placed your request with the Universe, and that the LOA is on the case. There's nothing more you have to do. Expect your desire to show up, and do your best to go about your day while feeling good. Whenever you start to stress out about it, remember that you've handed your problem over to the Universe and it's taken care of. It's not your responsibility any more.

Basically, when you let something go, you are cultivating trust. If you had a guarantee, perhaps signed by the president or God or your mother, that what you want is on the way *FOR SURE*, you'd have no problem letting it go. You'd focus on something else, and when the subject did come up it would only elicit positive expectation from you. Let this be the same. Letting something go doesn't necessarily mean that you stop thinking about it (don't obsess, though), but you do have to stop *worrying* about it. Choose to believe that it really is on its way.

✷ Poke and run technique ✷

One of my guides gave me this deceptively simple technique one night during one of my own meditations. When I meditate, I often translate the non-physical energy I connect with as my 'guides'. You can also interpret this energy as angels, God, your Higher Self, Source or whatever else resonates with you. As long as you are connecting to love and the answers feel really, really good, it doesn't really matter what you call it. This is a technique that works on a much more abstract level, which circumvents the mind's need to be fully involved in the process. For that reason, it does require just a little bit of trust and a willingness to stop telling the story of how you got where you are today, why it sucks so much and why you can't get out of it. In short, it requires that you be willing to back off.

When I coach a client, I stubbornly stay in a nice, high, stable vibration while they climb their way up the Spectrum (*see page 111*) to meet me. I bombard them steadily with positivity until they surrender. (I prefer to think of it as slapping them into happiness.) In this way of working, there is someone at a higher vibration, shining a light and helping you upwards. No one can pull you up, no one can MAKE you feel better, but you can be influenced by someone else's vibration. This is why sitting in nature is beneficial and why working with someone who has a higher (and stable) vibration can make a huge difference. When you're working alone, you can be that someone for yourself. In the methods of releasing resistance that I presented in this book, you do this by focusing on what you want before really engaging with your resistance. You can ramp up this effect by using meditation (*see page 232*) or any other technique you like to get yourself into a higher, better-feeling vibration on *any topic* (not the one you're trying to fix) before doing any kind of shifting work.

The higher and more stable that vibration, the easier you'll be able to positively affect any problem you want to solve. You'll essentially be shining the light of your higher vibration onto an issue that has a lower vibration. This weakens the momentum of the lower vibration (it slows down the Progression), and speeds up the process of releasing it. The poke and run technique makes use of this concept.

This technique is best used once you've had an anger release (*see Chapter 11, page 206*). Having a lot of stored-up anger can block this tool from working. Give it a try, though, you never know.

Here's the basic rundown:

Step 1: Raise your vibration on another topic

Choose any other topic that *already* feels really good to you. For a little while, totally let go of the issue you're trying to shift. Just be willing to feel better for a bit. Aim for the vibration of love. Now, you may be thinking, *How the hell am I supposed to find the vibration of love, if what I feel right now is depression?* Easy. *Change the freaking subject!* (I slap. But I slap with love.)

Is there anyone in your life that you love? A child, perhaps? A pet? A grandparent? If you have anyone in your life at all that you truly love (and yes, they can be dead), someone to whom you always give the benefit of the doubt, someone who could never screw up enough for you not to love them, someone who makes you feel better when you just think of them, then you can use this technique. Spend some time thinking about this someone. And when I say 'some time', I mean several minutes (I recommend three–five). Build a real foundation; this is imperative if you want this technique to work its magic.

Step 2: Poke at the issue you're trying to shift

Once you feel really, really good, and you're filled with warm, smooshy love, you can 'poke' at the issue you're trying to shift. What do I mean by that? Think of the issue you're trying to shift. There's no need to try and change your thoughts, you're not going to be here very long. Just activate the vibration of that subject. As you do this, you'll feel your vibration take a nosedive. You'll likely feel a physical sensation, like a sinking feeling in your stomach, a dizziness, nausea, etc. You're coming from a really high vibration to a much lower one. Trust me, it's going to be obvious.

AS SOON AS you feel your vibration start to slip, and this will only take SECONDS...

Step 3: Run

Wrench your focus away from that subject and bring it back to whatever person, animal or vegetable that allowed you to reach the vibration of love. This will not be the easiest thing you've ever done. Your mind is going to want to get into your issue. It's going to want to fix stuff and focus on the problem more. It will feel really unsatisfying just to dip in and then run away. But beware; if you get caught up in the momentum of the problem, you'll just give more and more energy to what you don't want. This is why I said that this technique requires some trust – you have to be willing to run, to go back to your higher vibration and not engage with the issue you're trying to shift.

Step 4: Rinse and repeat

Once you're firmly back in the vibration of love (which shouldn't take too long, IF you took the time to build a firm foundation in step 1), you can repeat the process of poking and running over and over again. Each time you do, you'll notice that it will get easier to go back up to love. The issue you're trying to shift will lose more and more of its momentum. Your vibration will take less and less of a dip each time you poke and your 'recovery' time will decrease.

Essentially, you'll be raising yourself up to a higher vibration and then, bit by bit, reaching down to pull up the issue you're struggling with. If the subject you're trying to shift sucks you in, if you let your vibration drop, you can't heal the issue. If that happens, just regroup and go do something else for a while, until you feel better. Then try again.

How long should you keep at this technique before you see results? I wish I could give you a specific answer, like '22.5 minutes! Guaranteed!' But I can't. It is a very individual thing and will change even from issue to issue within the same person. The first time I used this technique, I shifted a rather large and ugly issue within about 30 minutes (but I was kind of fighting it, because unlike what I'm doing for you in this book, my guides did not lay out the entire technique before asking me to try it. They asked me to trust them and just go with it, and I only saw the structure afterwards. So, I probably slowed myself down a bit). But 30 minutes of focusing is a long time, if it doesn't include step 1. Go for as long as it feels good. If you start to get frustrated with how long it's taking, you're no longer in the vibration of love and need to take a break.

Some issues take longer than others to shift. The deepest issues can have many layers. If you achieve ANY shift, let that be enough for you to celebrate it. Sometimes, you just won't be ready to let go of something completely. Trust that any shift at all will be beneficial (because it totally will be) and relax. Focus on how you feel. If an issue that used to make your stomach clench up with fear now feels like nothing (neutral), that's a huge achievement. You can take it to absolute elation another time. Remember, quantum leaps are uncomfortable, so don't try to take something from misery to love in one go.

Appendix III
Quick-reference Guide

Two processes you'll want to refer to again and again are 'Progression of a Manifestation' and the 'Five Basic Steps to Changing Any Belief and Releasing Resistance' so here they are again. (You're welcome!)

Progression of a Manifestation

Remember that all manifestations follow this Progression, whether they are 'positive' (wanted) or 'negative' (unwanted)

Stage 1: Focus on something of your choice

Identify what it is that you really want (always a feeling) and focus on whatever represents that feeling to the best of your ability.

Stage 2: Feel an emotion

As you activate the frequency of what you want, you're going to get some emotional feedback. The thing you're focusing on may or may not actually feel the way you want it to. If something feels off to you, if the emotion you're noticing feels negative, this emotional stage is your first opportunity to adjust your focus until it feels better.

Stage 3: Thoughts, memories and ideas

As you activate a frequency, you'll first manifest a corresponding emotion, after which thoughts, memories and ideas that match that representational frequency (or the same emotion) will show up. These thoughts and memories will give you more information on what the frequency you're actually focusing on represents.

Stage 4: Synchronicities appear

Synchronicities are smaller physical manifestations that represent a frequency to you but don't necessarily mean anything to anyone else. Validate these representations as meaningful.

Stage 5 to infinity: The physical manifestations grow

Larger, more obvious, physical manifestations will appear. This stage also includes action.

Five Basic Steps to Changing Any Belief and Releasing Resistance

You can, in fact, change any belief by:

1. Recognizing that your current belief is based on an incomplete set of data.

2. Opening up your mind to the idea that more data, much of which will NOT support your *current* perspective, exists.

3. Deciding which perspective you'd like to adopt (or just how you want that perspective to feel).

4. Looking for the evidence to support that new, wanted perspective.

5. Gathering enough of that supporting data so that you can accept this new perspective as 'truth'.

Glossary

Alignment: Resonance with a certain **frequency** (to come into alignment with…), but generally used to refer to the resonance with the frequency of what you really want and who you really are.

Anger: The feeling you get when you finally feel sick of the world beating you up, and you're ready to stand up and fight back. This emotion takes you out of powerlessness.

Appreciation: Simply seeing the good in what is in your reality right now.

Belief: An automated thought, opinion, decision or reaction.

Blame (blaming others): The feeling you get when you naturally turn your self-blame outwards, allowing the energy to flow out, rather than inwards (self-blame). Healthy when practised deliberately, constructively and *temporarily*.

Boredom: The feeling of being idle, of not allowing oneself to move forward. This feeling can actually occur at any point in the **Spectrum of Emotional Empowerment**.

Breaking Point Method of Growth: When we wait until a situation becomes too painful to sustain before making a change.

Celebration: Unconditional **appreciation** (appreciation on steroids).

Contentment: Neutral, with a slightly positive focus. You are no longer feeling pain, but there's not yet much pleasure. Not a state of **appreciation** but a more 'neutral' state.

Contrast: 'Negative' experiences that allow us to figure out what we don't want, so that we can use that information to figure out what we do want, instead.

Core belief: A general, underlying belief that governs how we form and interact with smaller, more specific beliefs.

Crappy Core Belief: A large, underlying belief that affects your ability to shift lesser, subsequent beliefs.

Cycle of doom: The cycle we get stuck in when we are attempting to move up the Spectrum but won't allow ourselves to realize an anger release fully. We simply let off a bit of steam and then revert to self-blame or self-loathing, pulling us down the **Spectrum of Empowerment**.

Deep depression: A feeling of numbness due to severely suppressed **anger**; of being disconnected from the self and the world. Nothing matters. Total **powerlessness**. Like lying down and letting yourself get beaten, without having the strength or motivation to do anything about it.

Denial: The act of unknowingly pretending to feel better than you actually do. People in denial are not aware of how they are actually feeling.

Discouragement: A lighter form of **pessimism**. You still trust the negative more than the positive, but you're not really sure of it.

Emotional group 1 (DEPRESSION): Like lying in the foetal position while life is beating you up. *See also* **Deep depression**, **Total despair**, **Total powerlessness**

Emotional group 2 (SHAME): You begin to bargain in order to get a little bit of what you want. Your worthiness comes from what you can do for others. *See also* **Fake gratitude**, **Guilt**, **Resentment**, **Self-blame**, **Severe insecurity**, **Shame**, **Unworthiness**

Emotional group 3 (ANGER): The most powerful and healing of emotional groups. You are starting to stand up and fight back, or remove yourself from the harmful situation. *See also* **Anger**, **Blame**, **Hatred**, **Jealousy**, **Rage**, **Revenge**

Emotional group 4 (FRUSTRATION): Just below the threshold. You can see what it is you want, but you can't quite reach it. *See also* **Discouragement**, **Frustration**, **Pessimism**

Emotional group 5 (HOPE): You know that you can have what you want, but you're not entirely sure that you'll get it. *See also* **Contentment**, **Gratitude**, **Hope**, **Optimism**

Emotional group 6 (ENTHUSIASM): You believe that you will get what you want and are looking forward to receiving it. *See also* **Appreciation**, **Enthusiasm**, **Positive expectation**

Emotional group 7 (JOY): You acknowledge that you already have everything you need to be complete. Life is awesome! *See also* **Celebration**, **Full empowerment**, **Joy**, **Passion**

Enthusiasm: The feeling of trusting that good things will happen and looking forward to them; usually less controlling than **positive expectation**.

Envy: A lighter form of **jealousy**. Pure envy is simply wanting something that someone else has. Jealousy without the component of scarcity.

Faith: A tool that allows us to believe that something will come about, even though we don't yet have a physical representation of it.

Fake gratitude: The feeling you get when you're trying to be grateful to some hostile power outside of yourself, either to appease them or because you've been told you should be. It's fake because being grateful out of obligation or in order to get something (even safety) is not gratitude. It's manipulation.

Fear: *See* **Severe insecurity** (they're the same thing)

Frequency: Always refers to representational frequency; the frequency that the object of your focus represents to you, what it means to you or how it feels to you – unique and personal to each individual.

Frustration: The feeling that you can and should receive what you want, but that it's just out of reach. A feeling of 'Why is this not working?' Also a sign that you are trying to take action too soon and make something happen.

Full empowerment: The *knowledge* that not only is everything always working out FOR you, but that everything happens in response to your vibration.

Gratitude: A 'lesser' form of **appreciation**. Appreciating what you have, but still being beholden to some outside power to some degree. ('I'm grateful that I received this from…') Not to be confused with **fake gratitude** or appreciation, although many people use them interchangeably.

Guilt: A feeling that you have done something wrong. This is often coupled with **shame** ('I have done something wrong because there's something wrong with me'), but doesn't necessarily have to be.

Happy Shiny Puppy: An infinitely joyful, playful, loving, open and authentic being who doesn't take life too seriously and is so happy that others become happy just by being in the same vicinity.

Hatred: Intensified **blame**, which happens when you've suppressed the **anger** and the urge to blame for too long.

Hope: A 'lesser' form of **optimism**. You are willing to trust the positive more than the negative, but aren't quite sure of it.

Imagination: A tool that allows you to visualize and feel the emotions of a scenario that is not currently represented in your physical reality.

Jealousy: The feeling you get when you want something that someone else has, and believe that because they have it, you can't. Belief based on scarcity (there's only so much to go around).

Joy: The feeling of being totally in the NOW.

Law of Attraction (LOA): The Universal law that states that any **frequency** that is activated will cause other representations of that frequency to join it.

Limiting belief: A belief that once served you, but no longer does, like an outdated software program.

Love: The feeling of focusing on something with only appreciation.

New World thinking: The paradigm we are moving into (from **Old World thinking**), in which we're primarily motivated by seeking pleasure, adventure, expansion and individuality. The main theme of the New World is pleasure maximization.

Old World thinking: The paradigm we are moving out of, in which we're primarily motivated by avoiding pain, staying safe, limitation and conformity. The main theme of the Old World is pain minimization.

Optimism: You are willing to trust the positive more than the negative.

Passion: The feeling of being totally in the NOW, engaged in inspired action.

Pessimism/negative expectation: A negative perspective, more trust in the fact that things will not work out rather than that they will.

Positive expectation: The feeling of trusting that good things will happen. Can be dampened if the expectation is too specific.

Powerlessness: A sense that random bad stuff just happens to us while there's nothing we can do about it.

Progression of a Manifestation: All manifestations, positive (wanted) and negative (unwanted), follow this Progression.

Quantum leap: Making an extreme vibrational change in your life: seemingly jumping from one part of the **Spectrum of Empowerment** to a much higher part of the Spectrum, although the change is, in truth incremental, if very rapid.

Rage: Intensified **anger**; happens when you've suppressed **anger** for too long.

Representational frequency: *See* **Frequency**

Resentment: The feeling you get when you are giving more than you actually want to give, doing things not because you want to, but out of obligation.

Resistance: Any perspective that causes you to focus willingly on something that doesn't feel good, and therefore blocking or *resisting* what does feel good, by making it seem that the painful option is the best-feeling option you have access to.

Revenge: Intensified **blame** (usually even more intense than hatred); happens when you've suppressed the **anger** and urge to **blame** and **hatred** for too long.

Self-blame: The feeling that everything is your fault, especially when others feel bad for any reason.

Severe insecurity: The world is a hostile place and you are not safe. This emotion spans the lowest two groups in the Spectrum (DEPRESSION and SHAME), depending on the severity of the insecurity. (Can you make yourself a little bit safe by appeasing others, or not at all?)

Shame: A feeling that you are wrong (as opposed to having done something wrong). You are bad in some way. Not good enough.

Spectrum of Empowerment: A positive and negative number Spectrum, where zero (Zero Point) represents the neutral point without pain or pleasure. The negative end of the Spectrum signifies the **Old World thinking**, where pain minimization is the main motivator. The positive end of the Spectrum signifies the **New World thinking**, where pleasure maximization is the main motivator. The Spectrum also maps out the emotions in groups as well as their underlying belief systems.

State of allowing: Letting an experience be what it is without judgement, concluding or deciding, or processing. A good mantra to help get into the state of allowing is simply to 'observe and experience'.

Total despair: A feeling of deep, overpowering sadness. One step up from **deep depression**. A feeling of being trapped and having given up on the idea that anything can be done about it.

Unconditional love: Focus on something with only **appreciation**, and without any need for the object of our focus to give anything back.

Unworthiness: The feeling of not being good enough.

Vibration: Often another term for **frequency**, either on one subject, or collectively (as in 'all of your beliefs add up to your vibration). One is said to 'raise' their vibration when it shifts to a better-feeling place relative to where it was before. It is not really accurate to compare one person's vibration as being higher than that of someone else.

Visualization: A tool to translate non-physical energy into something we can 'see' or engage with.